WAVERLY
Songs

WAVERLY
Songs
Poems

ROBERT SONKOWSKY

iUniverse, Inc.
Bloomington

Waverly Songs
Poems

iUniverse books may be ordered through booksellers or by contacting:

iUniverse
1663 Liberty Drive
Bloomington, IN 47403
www.iuniverse.com
1-800-Authors (1-800-288-4677)

ISBN: 978-1-4697-9169-2 (sc)
ISBN: 978-1-4697-9170-8 (ebk)

Printed in the United States of America

iUniverse rev. date: 03/09/2012

Contents

WAVERLY* SONGS

*"Waverly" refers in part to the resort, "Waverly Gardens"—a wonderful village with inspiring staff members, fellow residents, apartments, many amenities such as an indoor swimming pool and spa, well-tended grounds, flora and fauna, lakes, fountains, all therapeutic and conducive to the ageing poet's reflecting humanly upon his past life and present status.

Yet "waverly" also happens to mean "wavering" or "quivering" like the Quaking Aspen trees (*tremuloides*) growing abundantly about the grounds, or like me and my shaking hands—a life-long diagnosis of mild familial tremor. When the wind blows, the leaves flutter and shimmer a spiritual silver and green. They shake like a Quaker approaching his Maker. The cover of this book shows photos of Quaking Aspens growing at Waverly Gardens.

ACKNOWLEDGEMENTS

I am grateful to my friend Al Thiemich for the above mentioned photos, to him and others, such as Charlie Jacobs, Bruce Nelson, and Harry Camp for encouragement of the North Oaks Poets and Writers group. Delores Mixer has been my very talented co-chair of the latter. She and its many members, such as Jeanne Hanson, Cora Lee Richie, Ginger Davis, continue to immerse me in caring support and valuable reactions to my readings. In addition to the world's dead poets who influence me, I thank living poets I get help from these recent days, such as Stephen Cribari, Jim Moore, Don Chrchhill, Lou Klitzke, Richard Vallance Janke, and Joan Pierce. Others at Waverly Gardens and elsewhere who have helped my poetry are Dan Erickson, Chuck Dietz, Paul, Steve, and Mike Sonkowsky, Evan Millner, Gwen Goldmith, Andy Becker, Stephen Daitz, Jackson Hershbell, Charlotte Bailey Codo and others unnamed.

The names of others who have inspired me will be obvious in the poems about them; they are the bedrock of this book. And my wife Barbara is present as angel on every page.

LANEY AT TWO

If you play peek-a-boo
with Laney, age two,
her squeals of delight
and dimples that play
on her face take flight
immediately that day

from heaven to you—
giggles, wiggles that flew
from eternity you knew
before you came to earth.
For Laney even two years
could never wear out that mirth

rising from God, nor the tears
and tantrums of Laney at two.

MORNING

Morning,
    some buildings still twinkling,
      owls still hooting:
my angels think
    that, when I become ashes,
      they will sprinkle them;
but I'm still scribbling.

THE OTHER SIDE (PROSE POEM)

When I was a boy, there was a ghost in the attic of a house in my neighborhood. We could sometimes catch sight of it in the attic window. I knew then how scary and mysterious was the world beyond the grave. But I forgot about it, or repressed it, and, as I entered adolescence and became more "manly," the earlier feelings behind those voyeuristic goose-bumps of boyhood were tamed and received the usual ordinary habitations and names in various contexts, literary and religious. I grew up in Appleton, Wisconsin, a town that regards Harry Houdini, who promised his devotees he would communicate with them after his death, as one of its minor distinctions but is not otherwise outstanding for its otherworldliness. I was not especially superstitious or insecure about the next world. I'm sure I repressed even my curiosity.

Throughout the fourth year of my high school Latin course, however, I studied Virgil's *Aeneid*, and in Book Six I descended with Aeneas and his guide, the Sybyl, into the dark shadows of the underworld. Of course, we kids were struggling with vocabulary and syntax as well as the wonders of poetry and its rhythm, but when we hit the episode of Charon, the ferryman who transports the shades across the river Styx, I had an experience that was inexpressible then as now. Charon is a messy, red-eyed, filthy-bearded, and filthy-cloaked, deathless divinity, who is funny and yet scares the hell out of me to this day, and he presides over the water that separates the dead from the living.

Charon and his mastery over the waterways of the pagan next world sticks with me. Christian baptism by water, the archangel Michael, who receives and carries the souls of the dead across the River Jordan, as commemorated in the African American Spiritual Michael, "Row the Boat Ashore! Alleluia!," and the importance of water in other transition stories of world mythologies are richer and re-produce those boyhood goose-bumps because of Charon.

Five Haiku

1.

Flocks of finches flit
   up, down, and AT my window:
     the latter splatter.

2.

Jesse Ventura, The Seal

Jesse Ventura,
    the Seal, shocked the world—whiskered,
barks, looks like a seal.

3.

I do love my wife
    more than anything in life:
in death there's no strife.

ℰ❧   *Robert Sonkowsky*

4.

I live paradise
    on earth here and now, yes, in
Waverly Gardens.

5.

But who don't live here
    in this Kingdom of Heaven?
Sisters and brothers.

Five Non-Sequiturs

1.

6'4" 200 lb freshman

at registration says

"Ah ain't sahnin' nothin'

til Ah talks to mah mamma."

2.

Seven-year-old grandson's art on the kitchen wall:

former art-major grandpa says,

"It's museum quality."

3.

WALL STREET JOURNAL HEADLINES

"Record Profits and Bonuses, Corporations

    Pay no Taxes."

"Harvard Medical School says

    59 million Americans have no medical

insurance at least part of year; ca. 44. 000

    died this year because they could not

go to a doctor or a hospital."

4.

Blessed are the meek:
    for they shall inherit the earth.
Oxford study shows
    Men in positions of power
        have aggressive tendencies
            increasing when markets dive.

5.

WAVERLY WAVERERS (HAIKU)

Three-year-old blond boy:
Ninety-year-old gray grandpa
Says, "Careful, honey.

Elizabeth Juanita Hamm

Occupational Therapist

"Qui me amat, amat et meos canes."*

She said, "I'm 'Lizzi,' which rhymes with 'dizzy,'
and I AM," she said, as six others
asked her about their fathers or mothers
or spouses and she with beautiful smile
gave explanations;
and her assistants received her help and advice meanwhile.
Lizzi dizzy?! Actually, busy—radiantly busy!

In the therapy ward I sit opposite her in my chair
and become Fred Astaire,
while she directs my moves as Ginger Rogers—
I am envied by other old codgers—
I imitate her seated moves of toes,
feet, legs, butt muscles, to's-and-fro's
of upper body, moving lymph
up from each lower limb.

Then her hands, ah her hands, open
pathways of life's juice
from lower body into abdomen—
the hands of a skillful edema-masseuse,
massaging my limbs and lymph (and me) to heaven,
while chatting sweetly of her dogs and her boyfriend—
the lucky dog—and her garden,
blue-eyed therapist extraordinaire:
I become the dizzy one.
We are Ginger and Fred, a chair-dancing pair!

The Latin epigraph paraphrases as "If you love me, love all of me." I do.

Lizzi's Hands (Villanelle)

"As the sun was setting, all those who had any who were
sick with various kinds of diseases brought them to him;
and he laid his hands on each of them and cured them."
Luke 4:40 NRSV

Lizzi's hands are holy: they help, they heal
young and old, those who seek her therapy,
the earth, her dogs, her patients, all who feel—

she gives them her hands, her hugs, with much zeal;
digs gardens as her knowing eyes decree.
Lizzi's hands are holy: they help, they heal.

Her eyes are blue with that steady appeal:
centered, she looks at me and centers me,
the earth, her dogs, her patients, all who feel

her hands, her spirit: chrism of her seal
on our heads, firming our identity.
Lizzi's hands are holy: they help, they heal

us all, they sew, make crafts, make us be real
and in love with all of one family,
the earth, her dogs, her patients, all who feel:

from her garden she presents the best meal
a communicant gets eternally.
Lizzi's hands are holy: they help, they heal
the earth, her dogs, her patients, all who feel.

MENS SANA IN CORPORE SANO (TANKA)

Lizzi prescribed hugs,
    for my sanity, she said—
her most precious gift—
      it went to my heart and head:
      I preach it, gospel for all.

Unsound Science

"In a laboratory dim/ a mad scientist created him."

There once was a time
when *insana scientia,*
except for Adam and Eve
and except for Prometheus,

did not exist.
Today, however,
Mad Science

has come into its own:
the rest is refuse.

Eight Sonnets

1.

Dream Of The Rood

I dreamt I talked with a telephone pole,
an orb, the sun, behind it, radiant;
its cross arms and wires intertwined my soul;
galactic pulses, flashing, luminant.
Could crafted wood and metal enter hearts
Estranged from nature, beating cosmic beats?
Communicate with worms, with insect parts?
So many pathogens pollute the teats
Of Mother Earth and the animals
She nourishes to try to neutalize
The toxins, feeding neutriceuticals
to maggots, hugging bugs to sanitize.
My dream became an ancient Celtic cross
Embracing me, removing all my dross.

2.

Callipygian Eurydice Or Lordotic Eve And The Sparagmos Of Orpheus Or Mud Of Adam

Reality TV is artless stuff.
Apollo, Pan, and Dionysus flow
against auditions absent ludic show.
Eurydice's first death was not enough:
as poet Orpheus, charming Pluto gruff,
looked back, Eurydice returned below,
like Eve undone by serpent unto woe
when husband Adam saw her in the buff.
Their sin was not barenakedness but pride.
Their punishment was sexuality.
Then Orpheus loved boys exclusively.
So jealous Maenads tore apart his hide.
His severed head proclaims we humans crib
from Eve's extra vertebra, not Adam's rib.

3.

HOMECOMING: A TRUNCATED SONNET

A loud single shot, unanswered, woke
me from my dreams, at home on a clean sheet
in suburban America, not burned, but smelling smoke
of bodies scorched so you can't tell head from feet;
from waking memoirs of war that maims or lames—
real; yet from older dreams of boy-scout games
bonding us in adolecent dreams of lust,
and of merit badges—now lost in mid-eastern dust
amid the clank of tanks that blunts the screams.
The shot, outdoors, didn't wake Dad or Mom,
But to me sounded exactly like a roadside bomb—
No joke.

4.

PRINCESS SEMELE AND QUEEN MARY

Outside those gardens, look for love on high
delivered from that forward tilted spine,
a babe who grew up from a fruitful vine,
or purged to ashes, was born of God's thigh.
The babe is Adam newly formed of sky
and earth, and Bacchus, each becoming wine,
and having a mother of royal line,
of grief, of pain, assumed her not to die.

The cosmic spirit is a feminine flame:
we consume saving wine of sacrifice;
yet star of Mary's sextant must suffice
to navigate our sea and worlds aflame.

In death—in empyreal purity—
In our mother's arms we fear not to be.

5.

I Wonder

I wonder how my childhood home looks now.
Dilapidated? Bent and gray, like me?
Inside do wooden floorboards creakily
re-echo ghostly footsteps remembering how
my Dad and Mom would walk from room to room,
my little brother toddled everywhere,
his lighter treads yet registering his pair
of baby shoes, while I would thump and zoom?

Outside does sun still shine or snow still fall
on sidewalks, bushes, flowers, trees, and lawn?
Do kids still play around there? Are they gone?
I must go home, the very house, to know
by knocking on the door and pleading for
a tour of floors to stave my thirst for more.

6.

CHRISTMAS SONNET 2011

At Thy birth O Christ the birds of the air,
alerted by Thy love's power on high,
signal Thy entry as they dart and fly.
Horses, both wild and domestic, both mare
and stallion, galloping over the plain,
cattle bounding over rich pasture land,
all earth's creatures made by Thy Father's hand,
animal, human, know Thy love and pain.

And the angels who hover all around
want to sing to us and play with our souls,
energy force of God between earth's poles
and among planets and stars that abound.

O may we listen and hear them on high
in quiet as the Babe of peace comes nigh.

7.

WHEN I'M IN ETERNITY

For Catullus and Marilyn Taylor

Eschewing punctuation birth to death
on earth and, *faute de mieux*, I'd paragraph,
not sentence, seventy-eight years of breath
to tedious rigid structure, God's last laugh

on me. God's not a micromanager
but keeps his hands away and holds them high,
hilariously giggling distancer,
until collapsing breathless slaps his thigh,

exhales the Holy Ghost to comfort us
in misery and knows the final point
this joke will make as unambiguous,
no longer cryptograph or out of joint.
Celestial Editor please set me free
from autobiography to poetry.

8.

James Whitcome Riley made nice children's poims
'n' in'erestin' dialect stories,
but a dialect theory full of joims,
joims still infecting poet-wannabees,
who think they protect their integrity
using only their homeland dialect
never outside precious identity
given by God to His poets-elect.

Did it never occur to them Life's short,
too short never to explore other roles
than their virgin-birth and always abort
imagination's temptation of souls
as adulterous to their poetry,
thereby cutting it from community?

THE INSCRUTABLE

Some say life is how you spin it;
others, how you win it.
One friend will grin and bear it
only if he metaphors it
a satisfactory banquet,
not needing to abhor it,
finds enough selections within it
calculating how to sin in it.

Another will despair
because it's not fair;
she is so full of scare
and fight, yet doesn't dare
even muss up her hair
and bare anger in her stare
in her boss's lair.
It's as if she doesn't care.

I don't understand history or herstory.
All of the above is a mystery,
whether literally or cookery, or debauchery,
whether internally or maskery, slavery, misery,
or slippery sexually blustery,
or with me in a monastery or her in a nunnery.
It's all divinely providentially trickery,
which inconclusively is my discovery.

THE WOMEN'S MARATHON

She said she had never run
a full marathon in her life,
but at age fifty-two decided to go for it,
even though her previous training runs
had never exceeded a half marathon:
"The only muscular pain I experienced was in my face—
from smiling, I had so much fun, I was so happy."

LINDSEY PALMER (VILLANELLE)

Waverly Gardens Fitness Instructor

Lindsey, we sing of your power to heal
and your fine athletic ability.
Lindsey, you make our dreams of health be real

in water aerobics under your zeal,
as you teach precise moves with empathy:
Lindsey, we sing of your power to heal.

You swim, you run, you bike Triathlon's deal,
divine, but loving our mortality:
Lindsey, you make our dreams of health be real.

Goddess, you also can gourmet a meal,
tell us how you feed friends and family.
Lindsey, we sing of your power to heal

our bodies and our hearts as you reveal
your devotion and your sincerity.
Lindsey, you make our dreams of health be real,

and we reflect your love with warmth and feel
that we have become strong and wise and free:
Lindsey, we sing of your power to heal—
Lindsey, you make our dreams of health be real.

God's Kingdom Is Here And Now
(Villanelle)

We sing we're free, God's love dispels the night
for all of us as one at break of day;
God's Grace is in us, surrounds us in light.

The diverse peoples rejoice at the sight
of the morning star, Tree of Life, and say,
We sing we're free, God's love dispels the night!

Righteous people, beaten down by their fight
with evil yet continue in God's way.
God's Grace is in us, surrounds us in light.

The river of the water of life, bright
as crystal, flows from God's throne—yes!—today!
We sing we're free, God's love dispels the night!

There is no need for lamp or sun: our light
is the Lord God, who sends evils away;
God's Grace is in us, surrounds us in light.

God's kisses, more than bread and wine, delight
us here on earth, more than we could pray!
We sing we're free, God's love dispels the night!
God's Grace is in us, surrounds us in light.

Lovely Linsey (Tanka)

Lindsey's triathlete
    triumphs and culinary
extraordinary
     tales exercise our behinds,
     train our limbs, relax our minds.

WISDOM (TANKA)

Wisdom is planning:
    it's stuffy, hide-bound, pompous,
powerful; sometimes
    it's wiser to leap
    before you look: and walk on water.

WHO KNOWS?

An ultrasound of my prostate showed
a very dark center amidst the gray
swirl, concentrating in a black point:
the microbiologist did not know
if the cancer was boundless or not.

Was this a time of trial or evil?
I must know, dammit, so I pull back,
to my more usual shy vantage point
and telescope that black point as a black hole
among stars of heaven, and my death as light.

But the microscope said probably
the cancer had spread to adjoining
glands and vesicles, for radiation:
is this the famed "luminous interval
between dark abyss and dark abyss?"

The telescope replied that the light skips
black to bright to gray-between on earth.

Collateral Damage

In an interview before his execution, convicted U.S. bomber (and Gulf War veteran) Timothy McVeigh referred to the deaths of 19 children killed in the government office building during the April 1995 Oklahoma City bombing as "collateral damage".

"the civilian to soldier death ratio in wars fought since the mid-20th century has been 10:1."—Wikipedia

Deaths for the Greater Good—
    Hiroshima, Nagasaki, My Lai, Nanking, Texas Death Row, Red Sea—
        authorities say are Just and Righteous.
Turn the other cheek.

THREE HAIKU

1.
Our drones overhead,
    suicide bombers below:
Whose side is God on?

2.

The old recruiters
      of the young, who die: "We old
live on—recruit more."

3.

Amazon dot com
    is not a woman *manqué,*
but shoots everything.

A Crown Of Sonnets
(Seven Concatenated Sonnets)

Skip Gibson

Richard Vernon "Skip" Gibson
August 9, 1940-May 27, 2010

". . . the fruit of the spirit is love, joy, peace.
patience, kindness, generosity, faithfulness,
gentleness, and self-control." Galatians 5:22-23

The Crown*
Sonnet 1

Deign to accept, O Lord, this crown of praise
to celebrate Your servant, Skip Gibson;
He traveled far, suffered much, served Your Son,
spreading joy, never quitting, all his days,
never swerving from his duties, in love
of neighbors, of enemies, and of friends,
until he lives even now and transcends
strength after former strength toward God above—
Man of varied tastes: pizza and ice cream
he liked and shared. To grand kids he was "Poppy."
His twinkling eyes endeared him to every
child and adult; yet under the esteem
pain increase spiritual intensity,
made his crown of thorns a crown of glory.

Sonnet 2

Made his crown of thorns a crown of glory;
he saw Ann, the first star in any crown,
when he was a college freshman, no renown,
and said at once, "I'm going to marry
the dazzling girl in the white ruffled gown,
on the way to the prom, crossing the street.
She's Royalty, we'll never dance, even meet.
Yet I'll persist, maybe meet her in town
after a game; she's Pep-band Majorette,
twirls a baton, many guys at her feet.
But I'll never make their grade of elite,"
he despaired, not knowing Your plan, not yet!
My own crown of laurel cannot compare:
Skip's, Ann's, and Yours are twined of loving care.

Sonnet 3

Skip's, Ann's, and Yours are twined of loving care,
another triune mystery from Your
Providence to Skip's birth to Heaven's door:
baptism, second birth for the pre-ordained pair;
Skip's third birth Heaven decided
one day before Ann's birthday on earth,
a bittersweet celebration, not much mirth,
O Lord, but Your Comforter abided
with the family and friends who carried
Skip's body in an Honor Procession:
the pall with dove on top Chaplain Nelson
lovingly arranged him to be buried.
His aunt's pall, just a sheet with applique'd
dove of the Holy Spirit our faith stayed.

Sonnet 4

Dove of the Holy Spirit our faith stayed,
as it had Skip's, out camping as a boy,
age twelve, around the campfire led to joy
of Jesus. While His parents were delayed,
young Jesus, left in the Temple, conversed
with wise Rabbis. Jesus also was twelve.
They were amazed at how Jesus would delve
God's meanings and was in all Scriptures versed.
Skip went from that campfire to servanthood
forever: in school, at home, and in life;
later, faltering, strengthened by Ann, his wife,
together throughout the world they'd do good,
in Bolivia and El Salvador.
Yet at age fifteen Skip was to live no more.

Sonnet 5

Yet at age fifteen Skip was to live no more:
the surgeon said bone cancer gave no chance
beyond one per cent to survive and prance
on the football field he loved, or dance floor.
But Skip persisted beyond one per cent,
with prosthesis for amputated leg,
baffling the doctors, who could never beg
misdiagnosis but claim intent.
From pain to strength, Skip limped up to the top
of the challenging investment business,
and when scape-goated in the nineties mess,
frustrating misunderstanding did not stop
Skip: now he drew upon the deepest love
from family, and friends, and God above.

Sonnet 6

From family, and friends, and God above
supportive love redounded and returned
to Skip and Ann far beyond what they earned;
for the grace of God had infused their love
with purest sacrificial Christian wine
empowering their travels to volunteer
both near and far to free the poor from fear,
hopeless homelessness, hunger: all could dine
on Your symbols of worship, other gifts
of earthly food, housing, and skills for life—
this mission and burning purpose was rife
in their acts and thoughts that Your Spirit lifts.
You, O Lord, helped and were Skip's strength, for him
to leave memories that never grow dim.

Sonnet 7

To leave memories that never grow dim:
near the end cancer invaded Skip's brain;
medical help dispelled some of the pain;
death threatened to take more than the lost limb.
At Waverly Gardens there did descend
the dove of peace upon the struggling man
whose strength was those many, and beauteous Ann,
at his bedside; all awaited the end,
resigned, in perfect faith and peace, when lo!
to provide them one more gift, Skip Gibson,
happily persistent, woke like the sun
of morning, drank liquids; he loved us so;
gave smiles, jokes, spirit to remember always.
Deign to accept, O Lord, this crown of praise.

Nach Heim

As I age O God I am more alone.
Take me home. Take me home.

O my Lord, I seek your face.
I find you only by grace
Of friends loving giving.
As I age O God I am more alone.
Take me home. Take me home.

My endless flow is dear and sweet.
Yet I long for You to meet
me in the land of the living.
As I age O God I am more alone.
Take me home. Take me home.

To comfort my family
help my dear ones outlive me.
I miss my Mom and Dad.
As I age O God I am more alone.
Take me home. Take me home.

Forever mourning playmates
from those days, and girls on dates,
and all childhood friends who have died,
as I age O God I am more alone.
Take me home. Take me home.

Three Farewells

1

In Praise Of Waverly Gardens And Alane Davies

At Waverly Gardens Hail to our Alane!
She saved us all from many a pain,
making Waverly a paradise for the retiree,
performing many roles, a multi-tasker,
allowing old residents gracefully
to lose our minds: all of us wanted to ask her
to stay, continuing twenty-four-seven,
slaving day after day for us,
but we were selfish; and her new job will be heaven:
more time for her daughter, new ways to grow.
With weaker mind, thus stronger heart, I pled,
"Alane, we need you; please don't go!"
She promised to keep us in her heart and head;
so Hail to Our Alane! Farewell!
In our prayers with your new work we know you'll excel!

2.

Cassie Pojanowski, Wellness Instructor
A Sonnet For St. Cassie

Cassie, when you leave Waverly Gardens
as leader of Arthritis Aerobics,
we'll see these lovely grounds through the sad lens
of missing your magnificent athletics,

your ballet moves, and your Hokey Pokey—
all done with love: I promise not to cry;
we'll get by; we'll make do with memory
of body, voice, and smile floating us high.

Goodbye, we wish you well in your career,
your studies, and the fullness of your life,
for which we'll pray whether you're far or near,
whether you consent to become a wife

yourself, lead Hokey Pokies at others' weddings,
or find still more ways to bring God's blessings.

3.

Eileen Duffy, Resident

Goodbye, Eilene, goodbye, Eileen,
you are our queen,
I'll see you on my computer screen.

TWO MORE HAIKU

1.

MORNING AFTER
NEW YEAR'S PARTY

At twelve went to bed,
    should have gone at nine I whine:
wine's throbbing my head.

2.

New Year's Resolution

Bring home from Iraq
    our experts; declare war on
ourselves; get roads back.

THE WORLD CLICKS

It ticks as a clock or a heart, in sync
as flamenco heels' xylophonic pace.

Time gallops you gallop we gallop all three
into midnight of war or dawn of peace.

Whoppety whoppety of helicopters,
or tap, tap, tap of tap-dancers' toes.

Click click of heels and of roulette wheels,
hippety hop to the barber shop.

The snippety snip of clippers,
The zippety zip of zippers.

Buttons unbuttoned from buttonholes,
One by one, or ripped from souls

of life on streets or in any shacks
where dogs will nip fleas or hind-foot scratch.

Chirps of crickets or cicadas quick
as castanets or solar cyclic:

staccato metronomical,
lickety-split astronomical.

The pelting of hail, sleet, rain,
hard, medium, soft, to entrain

pistons in engines declining in cars,
snapping unsnapping of snaps of scars.

Crickets' chirps and drummers' sticks
click so perfectly time itself

slows away from the station,
clickety-clack echoing back.

Pulsing blips on the screen.
Ah-doo-dah

day.

ANGELS

I love the littlest angels, those
dancing on a pin point,
and I adore the huge motherly ones,
those so big you think their toes
alone might reach your nose
or go out of joint
and succumb to tons.

HARRY CAMP (VILLANELLE)

Your vision will outlive every tree,
even the Tree of Life, sprouting anew,
O Harry Camp, master of forestry.

Your Tree of Life is your wife, happily:
she does the work of a whole forest crew.
Your vision will outlive every tree.

Myrna makes your so-called retirement be
a time for your work and plans to renew.
Your vision will outlive every tree.

Its brightness lit your way infinitely
spanning the world's forests all but a few.
Your vision will outlive every tree.

At each camp you got and told many a story—
to each, both mirth and community glue.
O Harry Camp, Master of forestry.

Your vision will outlive every tree,
O Harry Camp, Master of forestry.

DEBBIE CRUMB (TANKA)

Presbyterian Homes Staff

Cleans our place Wednesdays,
    far more than a housekeeper:
loving friend and aide,
    always over and above,
    up-beat, prays for us with love.

STILL MORE HAIKU

1.

GERI GALLAGHER
Staff Waverly Gardens

Debbie's friend, sweet nurse,
    gorgeous, has many duties,
but always hugs me.

2.

CHAR VALTERS, WAVERLY GARDENS STAFF

Musician, artist,
    our front desk receptionist,
she knows all, runs all.

3.

ROGGI
Staff Waverly Gardens

Waiter, cook, singer
    better than Perry Como,
proud Filipino!

4.

KATHY RANEY
RN AgeWell Home Care

Lively, full of zeal,
    close friend, nurse to us weekly.
We share her with Kings!

5.

GINA CINCINNELLI
Physicians Assistant

Better than doctors,
      more beautiful than
Lolobrigida!

REMEMBERING MISS MALARKEY:

A Poet's Autobiography

My first love was my second-grade teacher,
Miss Malarkey, so pretty and petite;
I was seven, a puppy, at her feet;
her spelling lessons made me her creature,
filling my head making it swim over the brim;
"Use the words," she ordered, "in stories and verse."
I wrote her a poem about a MONSTER, or WORSE:
"In a laboratory dim/ a mad scientist created him."

Seventy years later I remembered those lines
And drew "insane," then "unsound" from "mad'
to title my book *Unsound Science*—Not bad!
I'm writing my next amid flowers and vines
at Waverly Gardens: *Waverly Songs.*
Miss Malarkey, intercede for this old sinner's wrongs.

CONTENTS

INTRODUCTION

It was more than we expected and nothing for which we could completely prepare. In 2010, I was appointed to serve a United Methodist congregation 150 miles from my home in southern Nevada. Having spent more than two decades in the Las Vegas valley, serving four congregations and as a district superintendent, I knew my options for staying in the area were limited when appointments were being set by the Cabinet.

Until this appointment, my wife, Marilyn, acted as the trailing spouse. Moving from one side of town to the other, leaving her position for two years when I was appointed to a church in Arizona, and then returning with me to southern Nevada, she followed wherever I was sent. By the time of my appointment in 2010, she was well established in a corporate position as the vice president of compensation for a major international company. Anyplace I would move within our annual conference would not provide an equivalent position for her. As retirement within a few years was an option for me, we made the difficult decision to live in a commuter marriage.

This book comes out of our two years of living apart and the experiences of other clergy couples who, for sundry reasons, decide to live in separate homes for a season.

I begin with an understanding of the nature of covenant as it relates to God, marriage, and ordination. Then, in the first major section, I explore the decision-making process and intricacies of accepting an appointment that causes a geographical separation. The second section deals with the first days of living apart, making your house a home, and intimacy issues. In the third section, I look at coming home, reuniting, and creating a new life together. Marilyn writes the fourth section from her perspective on our commuter marriage. In the final section, I add a few concluding remarks.

I sincerely appreciate the support of my wife and of the old and new friends who accompanied me along this journey. Also, the experiences shared by other commuting couples brought clarity to what needed to be written and are greatly appreciated.

PEOPLE OF MANY COVENANTS

ovenant is not a common concept in church circles, much less in the general population. While related to a promise or contract, which people understand, a covenant has a greater depth of meaning and application, particularly in a biblical context. Promises and contracts are binding agreements between parties; covenants go beyond agreements and bring the parties into relationship with each other.

When my wife and I purchased our home, we signed a sales agreement setting the price and terms of purchase. Everything was explicitly stated and legally binding. Signing the contract, we bonded ourselves to uphold the agreement, but not to have a relationship with the seller. We never met her, never spoke to her, and negotiated everything through our real estate agent. It was an impersonal, detached process.

When we enter into covenants, we commit to ongoing relationships with the other parties. God enters into covenant with us. It began in the garden of Eden. In creating Adam and Eve, God entered into relationship with them. God breathed into them the breath of life and the Spirit, bringing them alive and committing to be in relationship with them. Even when they broke that relationship, God sought them in the garden, desiring to restore what had been severed. It's the first demonstrative good news of God's covenant with us.

Covenant language is evident throughout the scriptures. God makes a covenant with Noah and his sons in Genesis chapter nine. More familiar is God's fourfold covenant relationship with Abraham in Genesis chapters fifteen and seventeen. God promises to make Abraham the "ancestor of a multitude of nations"[1]; "to be God to you and to your offspring after you"[2]; to "give to you, and to your offspring after you, the land where you are now an alien, all the land of Canaan,"[3]; and to require in return that "every male among you shall be circumcised."[4]

Ultimately, God enters into a covenant with us through Jesus Christ. Desiring to be in temporal and eternal relationship with us, God sent Jesus to mend the brokenness caused by sin and to redeem us. Jesus uses covenant language in the institution of the Lord's Supper: "Then he took a loaf of bread, and when he had given thanks, he broke it and gave it to them, saying, 'This is my body, which is given for you. Do this in remembrance of me.' And he did the same with the cup after supper,

---

[1] Genesis 17:4.

[2] Genesis 17:7.

[3] Genesis 17:8.

[4] Genesis 7:10.

saying, 'This cup that is poured out for you is the new covenant in my blood.'"[5]

God has entered into a covenant with us, and claims and calls us God's own. God's covenant is not only descriptive of what God will do, but also what God requires of those who enter into this relationship. God requires that we fulfill our obligation: "The first is, 'Hear, O Israel: the Lord our God, the Lord is one; you shall love the Lord your God with all your heart, and with all your soul, and with all your mind, and with all your strength.' The second is this, 'You shall love your neighbor as yourself.' There is no other commandment greater than these."[6] Covenants flow in both directions between those in the relationship.

Not only do we have a covenant with God, we also enter into other sacred covenants that emerge from our relationship with God. One of those covenants is the commitment and relationship we have with our spouses. While marriage can be understood in the legal terms of a contract between two people, in the Judeo-Christian tradition, it is a covenant willingly entered into by two people. The wedding vows use the relational language of loving, honoring, and cherishing each other rather than the legal jargon of contractual, binding agreements. Next to our covenant with God, marriage is the most solemn, holy covenant we make in life.

The ritual begins with the acknowledgment that people gather in the presence of God, who is the author

---

[5]   Luke 22:19–20.

[6]   Mark 12:29–30.

of the covenant of marriage. Charged to recall the holy covenant into which they are entering, the groom and the bride state the covenant to each other: "I, _____, take you, _____, to be my wife/husband, to have and to hold, from this day forward, for better, for worse, for richer, for poorer, in sickness and in health, to love and to cherish, for the rest of my life. This is my solemn vow." Wedding rings, symbols signifying the solemnity of the covenant, are usually then exchanged. A declaration of marriage by the officiant confirms the covenant made between the couple.

The importance and significance of the marriage covenant is evident throughout Scripture. While marriage at times solidified treaties and assured economic security, it was considered a holy commitment, paralleling the relationship between God and God's people. In the Hebrew Testament, Israelite men were prohibited from marrying foreign women and divorce was highly restricted, because both were considered breaches of the covenant with God.

In the Christian Testament, when challenged on the issues of marriage and divorce, Jesus teaches that a man is not to divorce his wife, as what God joined together, no one is to separate. While acknowledging the reality of divorce in his day, Jesus understands it as a concession and a breaking of covenant, rather than as an open option for believers.

The early church leader, Paul, gave the first believers instructions on marriage and restated the prohibition against divorce. He also uses the analogy of marriage to represent the relationship between Jesus and the Church.

Marriage was and is a holy covenant that ties people to each other and is to reflect the love and nature of our relationship to God.

Another important covenant for clergy is their vow to serve God. As individuals called from among the people of God, clergy have a sacred covenant with God, the people, and other ordained clergy. In the United Methodist tradition, that covenant is expressed in this way: "Ordained persons exercise their ministry in covenant with all Christians, especially with those whom they lead and serve in ministry. They also live in covenant of mutual care and accountability with those who share their ordination, especially in the United Methodist Church, with the ordained who are members of the same annual conference and part of the same Order."[7] This covenant connects clergy to the communities they serve and to each other through the Order of Elders, Order of Deacons, or association of local pastors. The purpose of the Orders is to provide "for continuing formation is relationship to Jesus Christ," "develop a bond of unity," and "for mutual care and accountability."[8] This covenant, like others, is a sacred trust.

In the grand design for clergy and their families, these covenants are to work in harmony with each other. One's relationship with God is primary; it steers and sustains the other relationships. Marriage is not in conflict with one's relationship with God, but rather

---

[7]   *The Book of Discipline of the United Methodist Church—2008,* para. 303.3.

[8]   *The Book of Discipline,* para. 307.

is an expression of that covenant. Similarly, one's relationship to God is integral to ordination and is to work in concert with one's commitment in marriage. All three covenants need to seamlessly interact to maintain a vital relationship with God, a happy marriage, and a fulfilling ministry.

In some cases though, these covenants can conflict when serving a particular church requires the pastor to relocate and separate from family. The tension arises from a desire to remain faithful to one's calling as a disciple of Jesus Christ, to maintain a meaningful and intimate relationship with one's spouse, and to keep covenant with other clergy to serve where needed. In making the decision to relocate without family, it may feel as though one must choose between being faithful to God and ordination and being faithful to one's family. This is how conflict in the covenants can arise, particularly if the clergy spouse feels marginalized or resentful of the process that asks the pastor to relocate.

In the United Methodist Church, clergy are appointed by a bishop and accept the discernment and decision of the bishop to serve where needed. While taking a voluntary leave of absence is an alternative to accepting a church assignment, requesting a leave is sometimes perceived as a lack of commitment to the process and fellow clergy. If the pastor and/or the pastor's spouse feel powerless in the decision-making process that results in a geographical separation, resentment can arise.

In a survey I conducted of clergy and spouses in the United Methodist Church who were or had been in commuter marriages,[9] I discovered expressions of resentment toward the bishop and the appointment process. In most of the instances, the clergy felt their options were limited, particularly when they had previously declined a change in appointment for personal reasons. Several explored an "out," whether by doing ministry beyond the local church, transferring to another region, or even changing careers, but found these were not viable options at their age and station in life. They then accepted the appointment discerned by the bishop.

Although there was no expression of resentment toward God, some wondered whether God had directed this decision. In responding to a survey question about the relatedness of our God, marriage, and ordination covenants, one spouse said, "I don't know why we are separated. But I am a witness to God's faithfulness to each of us as we continue to support each other from afar." Another spouse, when asked how his relationship had changed, said, "My relationship changed greatly. I felt abandoned." A clergy member commented, "I am still struggling to understand what this is all about, what my role should be, and how to make the best of it." Another admitted, "My relationship with God probably got worse because of depression and inattention." There were an

---

[9]   Clergy and spouses in the Desert Southwest Annual Conference of the United Methodist Church previously or currently geographically separated due to the clergy member's church assignment were invited to complete an online survey. The results and comments were compiled and appear in several sections of this book.

equal number, however, who felt that their relationships with God had not changed or were strengthened by needing to rely more on God.

As choosing to live apart can result in dissonance at many levels, careful consideration of the variables is required before making the decision.

Talking Through It

How do you understand *covenant* related to your relationship with God, your spouse, and your service in the kingdom of God?

For you, how might these covenants conflict with one another?

How do you prioritize these covenants when considering a commuter marriage?

SECTION ONE

LIFE TOGETHER

A Difficult Choice

Making the decision to live apart sometimes feels like wrestling with an angel. Like Jacob, you want the blessing of the Lord by doing what God requires of you, but coming to the conclusion that as a couple you will live at two separate addresses doesn't come easily. Some weigh the pros and cons, but others feel the decision is already made and they must simply comply.

That was the case for John and Joyce. In his previous assignment, although John gave a hundred-and-ten percent of himself, the congregation failed to thrive. When it came time for evaluation, the bishop determined that John needed a different assignment and offered John a part-time position in a church located in a county more than 150 miles from his home. Struggling to make ends meet and with Joyce as the principle breadwinner for the family, they decided John's only alternative, short of taking a leave of absence from the ministry, was to accept the new assignment, even though it was a significant reduction in pay for him and required his relocation.

Whether in the church or corporate world, taking a position in a different county, state, or even country is not always about career advancement or greater compensation. Often it is out of necessity due to unforeseen or unfortunate circumstances.

Bill was offered a church that needed his specific gifts for ministry. A strong leader, he had energized a rural congregation for nearly a decade and brought them to self-sufficiency, stability, and vital ministry. It was hoped he could do similar work in another rural church some five hours away. Having previously declined an assignment, he felt compelled to accept this position. While the new church and situation seemed opportune, the timing couldn't have been worse. In a declining real estate market, the home he owned with Betty wasn't marketable either for sale or rent. Further, their daughter, who had struggled growing up, was now comfortably positioned with her friends in high school. Accepting the new assignment meant leaving his wife behind to care for their daughter and to maintain the house. While the choice for Bill to move was clear, the reality felt harsh.

In any decision to live separately, there are many variables to consider and obstacles to overcome. For both John and Joyce and Bill and Betty, their decisions to live apart had economic implications. With Joyce the primary breadwinner and John needing to take an assignment where there were no employment opportunities for Joyce, the prudent decision seemed to be living in separate households. For Bill and Betty, who owned a home they couldn't sell or rent, it wasn't economically feasible for Betty to move. Although Bill was provided a parsonage with paid utilities at his new church, having two homes was a financial burden, particularly after Betty's employment unexpectedly ended and she was still unable to relocate.

For two-career couples, the decision to live separately is becoming more common. Whether justified by career advancement, economic security, or benefits eligibility, couples are deciding to have commuter marriages. We decided, for our future financial security and health coverage in retirement, we would live two and half hours apart, she in our southern Nevada home and I in a rural Arizona community. For other couples, it's a quality of life decision based on the family's need for access to special medical services, social networks, or simply stability. In all these scenarios, the common denominator and commitment is the decision to uphold the pastor's covenants with God and ordination without compromising a commitment to marriage.

With family and economic considerations and the continuing evolution of pastors as employed professionals, clergy commuter marriages will likely be more common in the coming years. Gone is the time when it is presumed that the pastor's spouse and family will trail after the pastor regardless of career track, financial considerations, and family needs. The family dynamic and system are no longer secondary considerations. Those charged with deploying pastors for service must give every consideration not only to the gifts and graces of the pastor and the needs of the local church, but also to the pastor's family dynamics and the financial, emotional, and social impacts of their decisions.

Talking Through It

What are your unique circumstances and needs as you consider living apart? What criteria are most important in your decision making?

What effects do you anticipate this decision having on your family?

THE BENEFIT-
COST ANALYSIS

A common business model and practice is a benefit-cost analysis. In making an investment decision, all the positive factors are discovered, identified, and quantified. This is the benefit side of the equation. Then the negative factors are compiled and value assigned to them. This is the cost side. The quantitative difference between the two indicates whether proceeding with the acquisition is advisable.

When all the positives are added together and all the negatives are subtracted, usually a direction is clearly indicated. The key to the accuracy and success of this model is assuring that *all* the factors and variables are included and analyzed.

In making your decision about living apart, you need to consider all the factors. A careful analysis is not a fail-safe method, because the benefits and costs can be neutral or circumstances may change after a decision is made. That being the case, the exercise is still advisable and will be beneficial.

Once when Jesus was teaching a crowd of people, he challenged them to consider the cost of being a follower. The people appeared to know the benefits: his teaching, his authority, the miracles, et cetera. Then he presented the cost: "Whoever does not carry the cross and follow me cannot be my disciple. For which of you, intending to build a tower, does not first sit down and estimate the cost, to see whether he has enough to complete it? Otherwise, when he has laid a foundation and is not able to finish, all who see it will begin to ridicule him, saying, 'This fellow began to build and was not able to finish.'"[10]

What are the benefits and costs you need to analyze and consider?

Some Benefits

While the difficulties of a commuter marriage are apparent, there can be some opportunities. During our two years of separation, my wife rediscovered her ability to live independently and manage many of the chores and maintenance I had routinely done before our separation. It did, though, make for some interesting phone calls.

One night my phone rang after ten o'clock; it was a somewhat panicked Marilyn. As she sat watching a favorite show on TV, her attention was distracted by something moving on the ceiling in the family room. To her horror, it was a large scorpion. With the house's

---

[10]   Luke 14:27–30.

vaulted ceilings, there was no way for her to reach the critter. Frazzled that a poisonous desert arthropod had invaded her safe space, she called me, not knowing how to kill the varmint.

Shaking the sleep from my head, I remembered that in the hall closet was a telescoping pole I used to change the bulbs in the ceiling light fixtures. While I remained on the line to provide encouragement and coaching, she retrieved the pole, put a rag on the end, and then thrust it up at the predator. Striking it and then unable to locate it, she wondered what to do next. I told her to take the pole, rag, and invader outside and leave everything on the patio until morning. Her adrenaline was still pumping, so we spent time together on the phone. I helped calm her nerves and assured her that the house wasn't completely infested with scorpions. Now she sets and regularly checks traps, looking for the intruders. I think she secretly does a victory dance with each capture.

In conquering the scorpion problem as well other challenges, Marilyn became more self-reliant. Living independently requires adaptation and some creativity. Resolving a problem and making independent decisions not only builds a sense of "I can do it!" but also self-confidence and self-esteem. Gregory T. Guldner, in his book, *Long Distance Relationships—The Complete Guide,* says, "Self-esteem flourishes in an environment that requires self-reliance, but also provides a secure relationship to fall back on when times get tough. For many people the LDR [long distance relationship] provides the perfect blend of independence and support to nourish self-esteem and personal growth."[11]

Another benefit of living independently is having greater flexibility with your time. As a compensation professional for an international corporation, Marilyn has a very demanding job that sometimes requires her to work long hours. While we were living apart, when she needed to work late, there was no sense of urgency to get home for dinner. Likewise, I scheduled my church meetings, appointments, and visitations on my schedule, without consideration of her timetable.

For some, this time apart also provides the opportunity to pursue personal interests. Reading, taking a class, picking up a hobby, creating a craft project, restoring antiques, bicycling, hiking, or kayaking are just some of the fun activities for which there can be more time. It also affords those with children more time to play, take trips to the park, and interact.

With your additional time and freedoms, there is also the flexibility to do things differently. It is particularly a good time to do some self-care and self-nurture. Besides classes and hobbies, you can establish more healthy eating habits, start an exercise program, or try some new spiritual discipline. This is your time to use as you choose.

---

[11]   Gregory T. Guldner, *Long Distance Relationships—The Complete Guide* (Corona, Calif.: JF Milne Publications, 2006), 67.

Counting the Costs

Often there is insufficient time to think through a decision to live in a commuter marriage. The opportunity is presented to the pastor and a commitment is expected within twenty-four to forty-eight hours. Much of that time is spent in prayer, seeking God's direction or, more likely, bartering with God like Moses. When Moses was told to go to Pharaoh in Egypt and demand the release of the Hebrew people, he tried to convince God he was not the right man for the job.

No matter how great the opportunity, when you are told you are being sent to a new church and realize your family is not coming along, there is a time of thinking that this really can't be God's will. As clarity comes that living apart is inevitable, there are many things to consider.

One of the primary considerations is your family dynamics. You need to find out if there are employment opportunities for a working spouse, the quality of schools for any children, and the adaptability of the family to a new environment. It's well known that children do not easily relocate, and it produces a significant amount of stress. According to the American Academy of Child and Adolescent Psychiatry (AACAP), "Moving to a new community may be one of the most stress-producing experiences a family faces. Frequent moves or even a single move can be especially hard on children and adolescents. Studies show children who move frequently are more likely to have problems at school."[12] Knowledge of the stress that relocation can cause a family, especially children, needs to be weighed against the absence of a parent from the household. Family life is significantly altered either way.

When the decision is made to live in two households, the remaining spouse and parent assumes greater responsibility for managing the household. The absent partner misses special occasions and life events with the family. If children are involved, school activities, productions, and sporting events are missed, experienced electronically, or narrated after the event. One pastor commented:

> Being apart puts a strain on our marriage. I feel very isolated and struggle not to get depressed. My wife is having to operate like a single parent and is overwhelmed by having full time work and caregiver responsibilities. It is hard to keep working on our relationship now that it is long distance. Unfortunately, the kids have seen the stress a few times in that we have argued in front of them, but we have tried to repair that so they don't have to feel the tension. We have also been frustrated by the lack of possibilities for my wife

---

[12] American Academy of Child and Adolescent Psychiatry, "Children and Family Moves," *Facts for Families Pages* no. 14. Last updated March 2011. *American Academy of Child & Adolescent Psychiatry*: *http://www.aacap.org/AACAP/Families_and_Youth/ Facts_for_Families/Facts_for_Families_Pages/Children_And_ Family_Moves_14.aspx* (accessed February 15, 2013)

and meaningful work in rural areas as opposed to urban especially in her field. We also hoped we would have more time to seek out possibilities for reunification of our family but it is everything we can do for me to keep up with the church responsibilities and for my wife to keep her job going and family.

Another consideration is the financial impact of operating two households. In our case, I rented an unfurnished home near the church I served. To set up a second home, we had to purchase everything. Even though we bought most items on sale or secondhand, by the time I moved in and filled the cupboards and refrigerator, we had spent more than five thousand dollars.

In preparing to set up a second home, it's important to make a checklist of everything you think you may need and then add up the cost. Are there duplicates at the primary residence that can be used? How will you pay for other items?

Once the second home is set up, there are additional costs to consider. There are utilities, cleaning supplies, and other consumable goods that need to be budgeted. Although it may seem obvious, don't forget the food budget. A challenge of living independently is coming up with menus and meals for one and buying accordingly. This is particularly difficult if one has only limited cooking experience and can't tell the difference between tomato sauce and tomato paste.

Another financial impact is the commuting cost. The distance and accessibility of your two homes determines the cost of each visit. For some, the only reasonable commute is by plane because of the distances involved. For others, however, a car is the only or the more economical option. With the commuting cost for tickets, fuel and food, there is also an investment of time that is lost while traveling.

The Basic Question

While there are multiple variables to consider in coming to a decision to live separately, there is none more important than the strength of your marriage relationship now. If you are struggling, the time apart may only exacerbate the problems you are experiencing. Absence will not make the heart grow fonder; more likely it will cause the heart to wander.

Even in a healthy relationship, the stress of living apart cannot be underestimated. As a couple, you need to honestly discuss the anticipated impacts on each of you, your relationship, and your family. Although there will likely be many unknown consequences, because you haven't been there and you haven't done that, you need to realistically appraise whether or not this is for you. The basic question is: can you do it?

One pastor, who was still living apart from his wife when asked what he had learned about his marital relationship, reflected, "We did not do a strong enough investment and foundation in our marriage to help it survive and even grow in the challenging times. I don't believe we would divorce but it has definitely challenged us and we haven't handled it well. We definitely have to change if nothing else because our circumstances have changed. We want it to be toward growth especially in our marriage and each other rather than the roles we have to play."

In making this appraisal, you need to be honest with each other and your supervisors. As you contemplate the options, it's easy to get into a "soldier" mode and passively accept your orders and apparent fate. It's also easy to underestimate the personal and marital impacts, because you want it to work or think you need to make it work.

Be cautious about trying to compensate for your visceral feelings or rejection of the notion of living apart with simplistic, spiritualized sayings like "God will see us through" or "We just need to have more faith." While those things are true, you can't use them to abdicate from deciding responsibly. There is no shame in saying that, as a couple, you can't do this, and in affirming your marriage covenant.

Emotional and Spiritual Costs

Not every couple can live apart for an extended time. When couples marry, there is the expectation that they will live together, sharing life's experiences. Even though each may have a career track with long hours and heavy demands, by living under the same roof, they are present to each other to process the day, give and receive encouragement, and enjoy each other's company. As one spouse put it, "At least I knew he was coming home at night." Living together, there is structured time, unstructured time, and simply being in the presence of the other without words. One pastor said that although he spoke daily to his wife on the phone and would occasionally Skype, he wasn't in the presence of her aura. Experiencing life together is more than sight and sound; it's smells, touch, tastes, and being in the same place at the same time. Deprivation of these connectors can be a detriment to an individual and the relationship.

Betty lived five hours from her pastor husband. Regular commuting was not an option because of work, raising a teenage daughter, and expense. Further distancing them was a lack of video capabilities on the Internet. Initially, she and Bill were very intentional about connecting with each other, but as time wore on, so did their resolve. Without Bill around, Betty felt isolated, particularly as their house wasn't in town. Church members who had regularly called and stopped by when Bill was their pastor no longer did so. She felt lonely, abandoned, and depressed. The emotional cost was steep.

The spiritual cost can also be high. An important concern is where the pastor's spouse and family will attend church. One pastor said that his successor welcomes his wife and children, but feeling uncomfortable there, she attends only periodically with her children or worships at a nondenominational church, where she can be more anonymous. On some Sundays, she drops her children off for Sunday school and doesn't attend worship anywhere. One spouse commented that when her husband relocated, "I pretty much lost my church family. I felt like I lost more than him."

It's difficult and even discouraging for the remaining family to stay at the church the pastor vacated. In more than a few instances, while initially welcomed to remain in the church, spouses were later turned away because church members deferred to the spouse rather than the new pastor for care. Being asked to leave was heartbreaking. After leaving those congregations, some of them stopped attending church, except when visiting their clergy spouses.

Ceasing regular church attendance was a remarkable trend in the survey I conducted. Whether feeling unwelcome, personally uncomfortable, or simply overwhelmed by the feeling of participating as a "single," several spouses didn't regularly attend a church in their community. One spouse said: "[I] gave up on church." For many spouses, separation resulted in spiritual disconnects. The cost of this disconnect is incalculable.

Your Perspective and Analysis

In commuter marriages as in life, if you see only the negative, it will be miserable. If, on the other hand, you explore the possibilities and pursue the opportunities for growth as an individual and as a couple, it will be good.

Tina Tessina, in her book *The Commuter Marriage,* presents the psychological concept of the *preparatory set.* While principally applied to people who stutter and their need to anticipate and control the pronunciation of a difficult word before speaking it, Tessina applies the concept to anticipating and better controlling general outcomes through visualization.

She suggests imagining every detail of your new setting and situation and writing them down. About visualizing the details several times, she says, "It will become ingrained enough to feel more comfortable and you won't feel so stressed about doing it."[13] In a section "Programming Your Attention," she adds, "By writing down the things you want to accomplish and visualizing them to make them clear, you can program that mechanism. Once programmed, it directs your attention to certain events and occurrences."[14] In becoming aware of these events and people, you will more likely achieve the positive outcome for the future you visualized.

If you visualize the best possible outcomes of your time apart, it will make the separation not only more tolerable, but more healthy and productive. The mind is a powerful determinant of outcomes. That's why the apostle Paul says in his letter to the Philippians, "Finally, beloved, whatever is true, whatever is honorable, whatever is just, whatever is pure, whatever is pleasing, whatever is commendable, if there is any excellence and if there is anything worthy of praise, think about these things."[15] In preparing to live apart, set your heart and mind on the life and relationship-

---

[13] Tina B. Tessina, *The Commuter Marriage: Keep Your Relationship Close While You're Far Apart* (Avon, Mass: AdamsMedia, 2008), 25.

[14] Tessina, *The Commuter Marriage*, 25–26.

[15] Philippians 4:8

affirming good that can occur, rather than obsessing on the negative. You'll be much happier!

Ultimately though, even with the most optimistic perspective, having placed on a balance the benefits and costs of living apart and prayerfully considered all the facts and variables imaginable, the decision is yours to make. Decide wisely!

Talking Through It

List the benefits you anticipate receiving by living apart. Assign a number to each benefit and order them from greatest to least.

List the real and anticipated costs of living apart. Assign a number to each cost and order them from greatest to least.

Take the top five benefits and top five costs from your lists and assign each item a value from 1 to 10, with 1 being the least important consideration and 10 being of utmost importance.

Add together the values of your five benefits. Add together the values of your five costs. Subtract the total cost value from the total benefit value. Do you get a positive number, zero, or negative number? A positive number indicates that you perceive more benefits in living apart. A negative number suggests that you have serious reservations about making this change in your marriage.

SECTION TWO

LIFE APART

CREATING A
WELCOMING SPACE

Making a House a Home

Where's home for you? That can be a casual question when meeting someone for the first time or a psychosocial challenge for a pastor and family. Just ask a preacher's kid or military offspring where home is and you'll get anything from a litany of places they have lived to an angry glare of frustration. They can tell you where they were born, but for most of them, that's not home.

Poetically, "Home is where the heart is" or "Home is where I hang my hat." For a commuting couple, the answer to the question is not that easy. Universally, we use the word *home* to define several places. I grew up in the Chicago area where my mother and two sisters still live. So when I travel there to visit, I say that I'm going home.

Home is also the place where my wife and I reside. Whether I'm returning from Chicago or just leaving a local grocery store, I'm also going home.

The real struggle for me initially when living apart was calling my out-of-state residence "home." When I was driving away from my home with Marilyn to return to my other residence, was I going home or just to the place where I lived away from her? I came to accept that I had two homes: perhaps not of equal significance, but nevertheless two places I could comfortably call home.

An important factor in having two homes is how you refer to each, particularly when speaking to the congregation. If you only refer to your primary residence with your spouse as "home," they may think you are not fully committed to being among them.

In my situation, I was very intentional in referring to my "home" as my residence with them. When inviting people to a meeting or gathering at my residence, I always referred to it as "my home." I thought this was important so that I was perceived as part of their geographical, social, and religious community. I didn't want to be perceived as an outside consultant visiting for a season, but as an integral part of the fabric of the church and community. On those occasions when I visited my wife in southern Nevada, I was careful to say that I was going to visit her, rather than going home.

Whether your second residence is an efficiency apartment, parsonage, or house, you need to make it your home. One of you is going to spend a lot of time there. It's not a hotel room you're renting for a week, where someone is going is make your bed for you, hang fresh towels, and vacuum the floor. If you don't think of your second residence as home, you may resent your arrangement and not adjust well to a commuter marriage.

Creating Your Joint Space

The very exercise of setting up a second home can be exhausting. In the planning phase, you make decisions about household goods and making your space livable. The most critical factor in this process is personalizing your home. Realizing that you are going to live in this second home for at least a year, you need to make it your own as a couple.

Marilyn and I chose to rent a house that we furnished. Having a house was important to us for several reasons. First, having not lived in an apartment for decades, I needed the space, a yard and a garage. Perhaps it was a mental health factor for me: if I was going to live as a single, I wanted to be comfortable, with many of the creature comforts I enjoyed at my home with Marilyn. I wanted the garage space to keep tools, kayaks, bicycles, other recreational toys and my truck.

Second, I wanted a house so I could meet with small groups there. Soon after arriving at the church, I realized that there was a need for a grief support group. Several in the congregation had lost a spouse in the previous year, and on my first official day on the job, I did a memorial service for yet another. Rather than gathering the group at a room on the church campus, I brought them together in the living room of my home. Sitting in my living room made the tearful, heartbreaking sharing more comfortable, especially with coffee and homemade cookies ready in the kitchen.

One other reason we chose a house was because we enjoy entertaining. Marilyn has an extraordinary gift of hospitality. Whether it was the Monday night group we hosted for dinner on three-day weekends when Marilyn was in town, or just another couple, we enjoyed having dinner with friends in our home. We wanted the space and comfort of a house for our ourselves and our guests.

Having chosen a house to rent, we began to transform it into our space. Although the house was my primary residence, she helped decorate it and gave it her personal touches. It wasn't a bachelor's pad, but rather a second home for both of us. When moving in and setting up, I not only brought my books, computers, and files, I also included items from my home with Marilyn that connected me to that place. Family photographs to hang on the walls of my office and decorative accessories for the living room were important parts of making both places home.

Probably one of the most significant things I did prior to Marilyn's first visit was to set up her space in the bathroom. I went to the store and purchased her favorite hand soap, shampoo, cotton balls, Q-Tips, hairdryer, hairbrush, and anything else I could think of that she regularly used, and had them ready for her when she arrived. In the morning, there was Half-N-Half creamer in the refrigerator for her coffee and some of the foods I know she particularly enjoys. In as many ways as possible, I was letting her know that this was her home too.

The transformation of a property from a house to home in a commuter marriage takes intentionality and time. Although the transition can be difficult, it is essential.

Community

Setting up a second home is not just the facets of furniture, fixtures, and feng shui. It's creating a sense of participation in a community. Home has positive, comfortable feelings associated with it.

When I visit family in Chicago, I'm not returning to a house where I once lived. The two houses in which I grew up are now occupied by strangers. My mother lives in an adult care facility and my sisters have their own houses. In returning home, I'm going back to a family connection that has some proximity to where I grew up. It feels like home to me because of the people and the memories associated with family, friends, and landmarks.

You can fill your second residence with all kinds of personal items, but it doesn't become home until you identify positively with the community and share in its life. The most obvious community is the church. For the pastor, integration into this community is expected, but unfortunately doesn't always happen. Having served as a district superintendent, I'm acutely aware that not every assignment is a match made in heaven. Moving the pastor again after only a year is sometimes necessary for everyone's health and sanity. Usually, though, there is a ready acceptance of the pastor into the church family.

While there is always the dynamic of the spouse's acceptance by a congregation and what role he/she will have, this is more acute for the commuting couple. Some couples, soon after arriving, catch wind that church members assumed they were having marital problems; otherwise they wouldn't choose to live apart.

For Marilyn and me, even after nearly two years of her standing at the back door with me at the end of worship on the Sundays she was in town, some people didn't realize that we lived in two different states. Maybe they thought that on the Sundays she wasn't present, she was elsewhere on campus or at work. Or perhaps they considered her an irregular attender. Some of those who noticed her infrequent appearances asked where she was. When I said she was at our home in Nevada, they were shocked. Sometimes I would explain that she lived there full time and tried to visit every other weekend; other times I would just let it go. Fortunately when she was in town, the congregation didn't expect her to do anything in the church other than to be supportive of me. How you and your spouse are welcomed into the church family has a significant impact on how you perceive your second home.

Another aspect of creating home is finding a level of comfort as a couple in the larger community. While we did not join community organizations and clubs, Marilyn and I found activities to explore and enjoy. I purchased a tandem kayak that we would paddle up the channel and along the shoreline of the lake near where I lived. Being hikers, we explored new trails and found adventures in a nearby state park. Checking out different restaurants for lunch and dinner also made for enjoyable outings and times. The more we did in the community, the more it felt like home to us.

Connecting into the community is essential to making a second home. Just as with transforming a house into a home, the more you invest in the life of the community and make it your own, the more you will feel at home. Home is more than an address; it is a lifestyle choice.

Talking Through It

Where is home for you?

In what ways can you create a homey feeling in two places?

How will you furnish and accessorize your second home?

In what ways can you make the new community your own?

FIRST DAYS

I remember it as though it were yesterday. For each annual conference meeting, Marilyn would fly to Phoenix after work on Friday night. I would pick her up at the airport and we usually went out to dinner with friends. Over the next two days, we had separate and shared meetings and activities. On Sunday, we sat together as the business of the conference was completed and then we worshipped with the other conference attendees.

On this occasion, as was customary, following worship the appointments were read designating where each pastor would serve. As my name and assignment were read, sending me away from her, tears streamed down both of our faces. Soon afterward, we made a hasty exit, not wanting to talk with anyone.

Usually we rode home in the car together, but this time was different. Instead of heading north to our home, I dropped her off at the airport and I drove the four hours to my new residence. The parting at the airport was nearly unbearable. I was sending my love home without me. That was the longest drive of my life, interrupted by stops to dry my tears and recollect myself. So began our two years as a clergy commuter couple.

The first weeks, even months, can be very difficult. There may be feelings of profound loss and perhaps anger. That which God joined together now feels torn asunder. Recognizing the feelings of loss, emptiness, bewilderment, and irritability as possible signs of grief is important to finding peace and wholeness in this time.

Grief is a familiar feeling. Whether it is the death of someone significant, a financial crisis, or leaving a comfortable setting for the unknown, everyone experiences grief as the result of a major loss. Grief is often accompanied by the inability to think clearly, act decisively, and function normally. Life can lose its meaning and purpose, beginning a downward spiral into depression.

ISOLATION AND DEPRESSION

Grief is often intensified by feelings of isolation and loneliness. Pastoral ministry by its nature not only sets clergy apart for holy purposes, but also socially isolates them. In surveys conducted by United Church of Christ and the United Methodist Church, seventy percent of the respondents said they had no one they would call a friend. In my survey of clergy who were in commuter marriages, every one of them said that loneliness was the most significant factor in transitioning to their new living arrangements. For nearly three-quarters of those clergy, not having someone to talk to added to the feelings of isolation and loneliness.

Feeling lonely in the ministry seems contradictory. The problem for clergy is not a lack of contact with people, but not feeling a real connection with them. Clergy are often known by their role and as a friend to all and not as real people. As one bishop in the United Methodist Church put it, "When I became a bishop, I lost my first name." For the pastor living alone, the isolation and loneliness is often more intense because when after worship, a meeting or social event, his/her church friends leave and go home, he/she goes to an empty house.

We are created for relationship with God and each other. In the Genesis narrative, God creates the first man as an expression of love, establishes a relationship with him, and provides him with all that is necessary to sustain life. In chapter 2 verse 18, it says, "Then the Lord God said, 'It is not good that the man should be alone; I will make him a helper as his partner.'" God then creates the animal kingdom, and Adam enters into relationship with them by naming them.

Although Adam has all the provisions for life, he has no one with whom to share it: his aloneness is not satisfied. To complete creation and a companion for Adam, Eve is given life. Adam exclaims:

"This at last is bone of my bones
      and flesh of my flesh;
this one shall be called Woman,
      for out of Man this one was taken."[16]

While acknowledging that single people are equally as whole as those who choose to marry, the veracity of the underlying principle remains: relationships form and sustain us. Whether we are single or married, our connection to others on a very personal level is critical to our wellness. As the writer of the Book of Ecclesiastes puts it,

---

[16]   Genesis 2:23.

"Two are better than one, because they have a good reward for their toil. For if they fall, one will lift up the other; but woe to one who is alone and falls and does not have another to help. Again, if two lie together, they keep warm; but how can one keep warm alone? And though one might prevail against another, two will withstand one. A threefold cord is not quickly broken."[17]

When we are isolated from our significant others, with whom we can share life's experiences and be unconditionally accepted, we become susceptible to depression. Back in the seventies, Leonard I. Pearlin and Joyce S. Johnson researched the correlation between marital status, life-strains and depression. Among the stressors they evaluated were economic hardship and isolation.

While some of their presumptions about being single are dated, their findings and conclusions are interesting. Measuring the degree of a person's isolation, they found that those who had resided in a neighborhood less than two years, had only one or no friends close by, and did not have a voluntary association with an organization felt most isolated. They observed a direct correlation between the degree of isolation and the tendency toward depression. "Being without a mate apparently leaves one open to the depressive consequences of life-strains, especially so

---

[17]   Ecclesiastes 4:9–12.

when one is also lacking alternative supports."[18] They also comment, "What we have learned suggests that marriage can function as a protective barrier against the distressful consequences of external threats. Marriage does not prevent economic and social problems from invading life, but it apparently can help people fend off the psychological assaults that such problems otherwise create."[19]

Putting Pearlin and Johnson's research in the context of clergy commuter couples suggests that not having your spouse with you, although you can connect on the phone and Internet, can contribute to depression, particularly in the early days of the separation. Compound the separation with not having friends nearby, the stress of the move and living as a single, and the strain of serving in a new context can add up to feelings of guilt, helplessness, and emptiness. These feelings are some of the indicators of depression.

Statistically clergy experience higher rates of depression than the general population and are at increased risk due to isolation and loneliness. It is important know and recognize the signs of depression in yourself and your partner. The table below is a compilation of commonly observed symptoms of depression.

---

[18] Leonard I. Pearlin and Joyce S. Johnson, "Marital Status, Life Strains and Depression" *American Sociological Review* 42, no. 5 (October 1977): 710.

[19] Pearlin and Johnson, "Marital Status, Life Strains and Depression" 714.

Rev. Tom Mattick

Physical	Psychological	Emotional	Social	Spiritual
Insomnia	Difficulty in making decisions	Sadness	Withdrawal	Difficulty in praying
Oversleeping	Irrational thinking	General unhappiness	Missing work	Sense that God doesn't care or is punishing you
Loss of appetite	Paranoia	Irritability	Intentional isolation	Desire to leave the church
Overeating	Slow thinking	Anger outbursts	Lack of joy in being with others	Questioning faith (severe doubt)
Weight loss	Indecisiveness	Feeling guilt	Avoiding interaction with family and friends	Feeling spiritually disconnected
Weight gain	Lack of concentration	Feelings of worthlessness	Precipitous arguments	Feeling evil

Physical	Psychological	Emotional	Social	Spiritual
Reduced sex drive	Self-degradation	Crying spells	Neglecting hobbies and interests	Feeling abandoned by God
Agitation	Thoughts of suicide	Feeling shame	Breakdown of family life	Loss of peace and joy
Headaches	Preoccupation with death	Feeling empty	Breakdown of friendships	Desire to curse God and die
Hand-wringing	Inability to remember things	Feeling of helplessness		Little interest in Scriptures
Fatigue	Scattered thoughts	Persistent worrying		Weary of doing good
Unexplained aches and pains	Persistent doubting	Feeling of doom		Difficulty accepting grace

Physical	Psychological	Emotional	Social	Spiritual
Lack of energy	Detachment from self	Hopelessness		Not loving God; not loving self
Excessive alcohol or drug use	Amplification of small problems			Feeling unforgiven
Slow speech	Planning how to die			Fear of judgment

Some of these symptoms may present simply as the result of moving and adjusting to a new lifestyle. They may well be part of the grieving process. If, however, these symptoms become more acute, affect your capacity to work or even function, damage your relationships, or persist longer than a couple of months, it's time to seek professional help. In Appendix A, I have provided several online inventories to help you assess depression.

Talking Through It

What major losses have you experienced in your life?

How did you work through the most difficult ones?

What might you do differently in this situation?

How might you overcome feelings of isolation in the ministry?

How self-aware and responsive are you to feelings of depression?

ADJUSTING TO
BEING APART

The first weeks and months of adjustment require special attention to self. Monitor your physical health. Eat regular healthy meals. Try to get seven to nine hours of sleep at night. Keep connected with God; use prayer, meditation, reading, and worship to keep this relationship vital. Find a confidant other than your spouse with whom can you be completely open and honest, and share your thoughts and feelings without fear of judgment. Find a support group; this is not a therapy group, but rather friends, new and old.

One of the saving graces for me was a dinner group. They started meeting years before I arrived. Eight to ten people got together every Monday night at a member's home. There was no agenda, no study and no singular purpose other than to be together. Soon after I arrived, the group welcomed me into their circle. I could be me. I didn't have to be the pastor or leader or convener. These people soon became fast friends who sustained me and I them.

Others are not so fortunate. Some discover that without a spouse, they are no longer welcome to do things with other couples. Perhaps it's the appearance of being single that is threatening to couples. It can also feel awkward to be around couples when your spouse is miles away; it is a vivid reminder that you're alone now.

Getting through the early days requires intentional work. Grief is not one of those things that time heals. Rather, the longer you let it go, the more deeply it roots itself in your mind, body, and spirit. If you just let grief run its course, it can become the guiding force in your life.

So what does it take to survive and eventually thrive in this new environment? First, be genuine. Faking what you are not truly feeling is counterproductive. It's not necessary to always appear in control and happy. I'm not suggesting that you let your sadness splash indiscriminately over everyone. When asked how you're doing, simply be truthful in saying that you are still adjusting and it's much more difficult than you imagined, if that's what you're feeling. Being genuine with your friends, church people, and especially your spouse lets them know you more intimately. If you consistently say that you're doing fine, even though your heart is aching, you betray your true self. You set yourself up for disappointment and the perception that others apparently do not understand or care. This further contributes to feelings of isolation and loneliness.

It is critical, particularly in talking with your spouse, that you be who you are and feel what you feel. You may be hesitant to share real feelings because of how you think your spouse will react. If you are having a great day and feeling on top of the world, there may some reluctance to share that with your spouse, because your spouse may not be in the same emotional place. There may also be some fear of triggering some question about your commitment to the marriage, that is, "He/ or she must not really love me because he/ or she is having so much fun without me."

The other side of that equation is the reluctance to share how miserable you are for fear of causing undo concern and stress for your spouse. While you best know your spouse, withholding your genuine feelings is not being true to yourself or to your spouse, and presents a false picture of your reality. It's okay to be who you are and let your partner be who your partner is. That's part of a healthy, intimate relationship.

Being genuine involves good communication. The key is listening. There's an old adage that says, "God gave you two ears and one mouth; use them accordingly." If you want to be heard, be a good listener.

Communicating over the miles is difficult. On the phone, you are trying to decipher meaning from the other person's volume, intonation, and speech rhythm. It's an inexact science. If you have video capability, you add the dimension of sight to hearing; however, it's easy to miss visual cues with only a talking head on your computer screen.

Good communication engages all the senses to interpret a message. Despite the limitations of distance, talking regularly with your spouse and children keeps those relationships alive and connects you to their lives. Share your experiences, feelings, and thoughts, and encourage your partner and children to do the same. These conversations can provide some healing for grief.

Finding a supportive friend or group with whom you can process your grief is also important. These are the people who accept you as you are and let you cry if you need to cry, laugh even when it seems inappropriate, and say what you need to say. They do not cringe in embarrassment or crumble under the weight of your sorrow. The very act of telling a trusted someone exactly what you are feeling and experiencing, without their judgment, correction, or need to fix you, is powerful and healing.

Stuffing your feelings down inside only results in emotional bloating and discomfort. Emotions need to come out somehow, and it's always better if they do so in a safe, supportive place and relationship.

Finally, during the early days, give yourself some grace. As a church leader, you continually extend grace to others. You accept their mistakes, frailties, and feelings. You love them, forgive them, and encourage them. That which you so freely give to others, though, you may often withhold from yourself. You can become your own harshest critic by thinking perhaps you should be above all this grief and accompanying baggage. Sometimes you may rationalize that if only you had a greater faith, you wouldn't feel so upset or lonely or depressed. It's just not so. People of great faith are not immune from grief. If you are to love your neighbor as yourself, so are you to show grace to yourself as to your neighbor. You cannot be fully gracious to others without first being gracious to yourself. Give yourself a break.

Talking Through It

What practices of self-care do you have in place now?

With whom (other than your spouse) can you openly talk about what's happening in your life and relationships? Name all of them. If you have less than three, your social network is too small.

How frequently do you connect with these people?

LIVING APART—
STAYING TOGETHER

He said it with some pain: "I hope you don't get to the place where my wife and I are, where it's easier to be apart than together." I had sought this colleague for advice when I knew Marilyn and I would be living apart. For several years my colleague's spouse commuted out of state for extended periods to be with family. Eventually she moved, putting strain on the relationship and making reunions more difficult. In her absence, he had crafted his own routines, and his visits with her became an uncomfortable interruption.

As the months passed for Marilyn and me, I began to understand what my colleague was saying. While I looked forward to her visits, each occasion required special preparation that was different from my regular routine. When I knew she was coming, I wanted to make sure everything felt welcoming and comfortable for her.

A significant adjustment was clearing the calendar of church activities and commitments so I could maximize my time with her. There were those inevitable weekends when I couldn't free my schedule, and we either participated in an event together or I did some church work without her. On those occasions, she would stay at the house and busy herself with reading, knitting, or just kicking back and relaxing. Her visits at times triggered an internal struggle between being with her and doing my ministry. While it would have been easier to go about my church work without her there, each time she visited, I needed to make the decision to affirm my marital covenant while keeping faith with my calling.

Every pastor faces that decision and tension. One of the realities of ministry is that the church will demand more of your time, energy, and attention than you have hours in a day. It can be completely consuming, leaving little time for family, recreation, or self-care.

Although there is always the struggle between time spent with family and time spent at church, when you live apart from your spouse, the conflict is more episodic and stressful. With limited visits, you may feel obligated to abandon some church responsibilities to spend time with your spouse and family. This can lead to feelings of guilt, as though you are neglecting your responsibility to the church. Guilt can in turn create tension and resentment of the situation and your spouse.

It may seem easier to be apart than together: out of sight, out of mind. One of the most difficult lessons for you may be accepting that your spouse and family must be a higher priority during those visits than a church activity. There will be emergencies and exceptions, but unless you make it a priority to spend authentic—as opposed to distracted—time with your spouse and family, your detachment from them will become more pronounced and problematic.

There is no need to make excuses for family time, fun, or self-care. If you don't nurture yourself and your family, you compromise the efficacy of your ministry. Your congregation, and for that matter your family, will learn more about God and love by your actions than by your words.

Another aspect of this tension is the grief couples experience when separating at the end of a visit. Parting can feel like a little death. For some, each subsequent separation becomes easier to accept. For others, though, each occasion is equal to or more intense than the last, causing them to question how long they can continue to live apart and whether it is even worth it.

To cope with the transition of leaving, couples often develop rituals. Although it may seem counterintuitive, in the hours preceding the departure time, some begin withdrawing emotionally and physically from each other. Anticipating the sorrow of parting yet again and not wanting to feel the intensity of that moment, they distance themselves. Some find that they are on edge, which leads to arguments and enmity. It feels easier to leave a spouse with whom one is angry. If the source of the anger goes unrecognized and unresolved, this ritual soon contributes to the deterioration of the relationship.

Then there is the professional posturing some couples do in preparation for leaving. They rationalize that each separation is necessary and therefore avoid feeling too much. Separation is framed in the context of a "higher calling" of ministry or as essential to achieving one's career goals. Like those couples who create enmity to cope, these couples detach and create space by staying in their heads and not their feelings. Parting is a duty to accept and not question.

At the other end of the spectrum are couples who want to make every minute count. Mindful of a deadline, these couples pack hours of living into the last fifteen minutes. Rather than distancing themselves, they remain emotionally, spiritually, and physically engaged with each other. They procrastinate and postpone the inevitable to the last critical minute. With hugs, tears and blown kisses, they finally go their separate ways.

Couples respond differently to living apart and coping with each departure. For some, it's easier to visit less frequently, because being together for a brief period is too stressful. Schedule demands, travel costs, and interpersonal dynamics can make for an unpleasant experience, and therefore they choose to be together less often. For others, the more often they can be together, the better.

You will need to find what works best for you, recognizing that your needs and circumstances may change with time. A change in your schedule at work or home, a change in discretionary travel funds, or even a change in health can impact how often you visit.

Whatever the frequency of visits and duration of stays, remaining a couple requires your commitment to maintain and grow the marriage relationship. Underlying every healthy marriage is good communication. Communication takes many forms, and for the commuter couple, it is the lifeblood that holds the marriage together over time and distance. Not living in the same space can limit communication unless you discover creative ways to connect.

Teleconnecting

In our cell phone, iPad, Skype, Facebook world, staying connected appears simple. Just speed dial, log on, or text, and another person is in your space instantly. It's a wonderful thing! However, ask any commuting couple, and they will tell you it's just not like being together at home.

Five months into our commuter marriage, Marilyn and I decided to downsize and sell our home. In the next five weeks, we sold our home, purchased a house and moved our household goods across town. Marilyn moved in and got settled. One night I Skyped her from my home in Arizona. Seeing the books on the shelves, the soft lighting, and cats on the couch, I said, "You really live in a nice home. I hope I can live there someday."

Although I was electronically connected and could see her in our new house, it wasn't the same as being there. I couldn't hold her hand, I couldn't smell the candle burning nearby. I couldn't taste the ice cream I knew was in the freezer. My sensory perception was limited to sight and sound, and even at that I couldn't see and hear everything happening in the room. I also felt disconnected in that where she now lived was not my home; I only visited for a few days at a time, and it felt more like a retreat than my home.

Teleconnecting is made easier by our new technologies, but has its limitations. One couple who talked daily on the phone shared their frustration with me. Not being able to see each other, they often missed critical cues and misinterpreted the conversation. Some things said in jest were taken as fact and felt hurtful. Lacking all visual signals, one partner would be uncertain how the other had received what was being said. When there were disagreements or hurt feelings, the conversation might end with one hanging up on the other. Even when a conversation had real closure, they couldn't hold hands, hug, kiss, and make up.

Despite the limitations, electronic communication is a lifeline in a commuter marriage. While meaningful conversation is important, casual chatting keeps couples connected as well. Realize that before the separation, not all your talk was on weighty matters and important decisions. You also talked about schedules, things happening in the community, someone you unexpectedly bumped into at the store, your aches and pains, and the partridge family feeding on your garden.

In one study conducted by Mary Holmes of Flinders University, she found that

"for both the women and men in this sample, talking and supporting each other seemed to be not so much about baring one's soul but about much more mundane things. Over and over again the people I spoke to talked about the importance of trying to keep connected to each other's routines. They wanted to know, not epic tales of past love and loss but what their loved one was having for dinner or watching on television, or what they had done that day."[20]

This is supported by other research that indicates "for some spouses at home, phone calls can provide a 'stabilizing experience.' The calls themselves, which allow the family members to connect briefly, are likely more important than the content. They signify reassurance and the existence of the relationship, and seem to be beneficial if the conversations are simply to stay in touch or to recognize special days such as birthdays and anniversaries."[21] Calling only when there is a decision to make or problem to solve gets the business of the relationship done, but does little for building connection. Use your time on the phone or computer to be in each other's presence as real people.

One of the nearly lost arts in our modern technological era is letter writing. Text messages, phone conversations, and e-mail have displaced the discipline of sitting down and thoughtfully committing one's thoughts and feelings to paper. Letter writing is a more personal form of communication, particularly as the reader sees the

---

[20] Mary Holmes, "Love Lives at a Distance, Distance Relationships over the Lifecourse," *Sociological Research Online* 11, no. 3. September 30, 2006. *http://www.socresonline.org. uk/11/3/ holmes.html* (accessed January 21, 2013).

[21] Laura Stafford, *Maintaining Long-Distance and Cross-Residential Relationships* (Mahwah, New Jersey: Lawrence Erlbaum Associates, Inc., 2005), 44.

sender's handwriting rather than a font on a screen. A handwritten love letter subtly conveys intentionality and a time commitment. Everything from the paper and envelope used to perhaps an added scent can convey special feelings of love that a message on a phone or computer screen cannot. Rediscovering this nearly lost art can bring romance to your communication.

Besides handwritten letters, sending your spouse a special gift or care package can communicate volumes. Perhaps it's some favorite, home-baked cookies, a bouquet of flowers, or something special to wear that says, "I'm thinking of you. I love you." The ways of remaining connected and intimate are limited only by your imagination and creativity.

Ordinary Time versus Quality Time

People make the distinction between quality time and ordinary or quantity time. Whether you're living together, teleconnecting, or with each other during a visit, you need both quality and ordinary time to build and sustain a relationship.

Quality time tends to be structured and contrived. It's making the most of the time available. The problem with quality time is it often restricts the freedom to simply be and to express. The sense of it is, "We will have fun and enjoy this time whether we want to or not!" Quality time implies no negativity, no hassles and no bad breath.

That's not how life is genuinely lived. We have our ups and downs, our good days and our bad days. To use a metaphor from the great philosophers, Shrek and Donkey, we, like onions, have layers; and yes, we sometimes stink. Certainly we need quality, maximized time, but we also need ordinary time that is unstructured and flows and ebbs with what's in and around us. That most often occurs with more time spent together.

Think back to the early days of courting your spouse. The first dates were mostly structured, polite and optimized for best appearances. As you spent more time together, you were more relaxed and more yourself. It was in those less formal times that you got to know each other and began forming a bond. For commuting couples, it is in spending time teleconnecting and visiting that those bonds are reaffirmed and strengthened.

Early in our commuter days, Marilyn would call me from the car on the way to her office. This was one of usually two times we spoke during the day. To signal the end of our morning drive-time conversation, Marilyn would say, "Well, that's about what I know."

One morning, feeling particularly detached and distant, I sarcastically but also sadly answered, "That's great! We haven't used up our whole five minutes!"

Surprised by my retort, she wondered what I meant. I had come to realize that we spent only about five minutes talking in the morning. I felt we were living in different worlds with very few points of intersection. Our conversation had become cursory and perfunctory, rather than caring and intimate. We were doing the business of the relationship without emotion or significant connection.

After that conversation, we committed ourselves to sharing more of the day and ourselves with each other. Quantity time is as important, if not more so, than quality time.

Visits

In anticipating a visit, it is important to be aware of your expectations. You may be thinking *honeymoon*, a time of fun and excitement, and your partner may be thinking *nap*. On the other hand, you may be thinking that it's time to make some serious decisions and have a heart-to-heart talk, while your partner is thinking it's time for mindless activities and maybe a movie. If possible, check in with each other before being together to get the pulse of your spouse's day, demeanor, and disposition. If you can't find a pulse, don't assume—ask.

Using the cellular technology in her car, Marilyn talked to me two or three times before her arrival. She called as she left the office, and we would talk about what kind of day she was leaving. I could anticipate her energy level just by knowing the time she'd left her office: the later her departure, the less energy upon her arrival.

In that initial conversation, we would also talk about dinner plans. We would first decide whether she wanted to eat out or at home; this was largely dependent on the time she expected to arrive. There were times when she got away late and grabbed a meal along the way, or when she just wanted to put on comfortable clothes and have a casual night at home. If we were having dinner out, I would ask what she'd had for lunch and what preferences she had for dinner, and plan accordingly.

Our second conversation usually happened when she exited the interstate. At that point, she had driven for two or more hours and was twenty-five to thirty minutes out. Depending on the difficulty of the drive and her fatigue factor, we would finalize plans for dinner, and I could anticipate her needs upon arrival. I would adjust my expectations to better align with what I heard her say she needed. It was always easier when we clearly articulated what we needed and didn't leave it to intuition or guesswork.

Flexibility in the first minutes of the visit is critical to a positive experience and can set the tone for the entire time spent together. Set aside any personal agendas and spend time reconnecting. Demonstrating love and care by listening and touching creates a welcoming, safe environment. The first few minutes are not the time to complain, present a problem, or criticize. Starting off on the wrong foot makes it difficult to get back in step. Make the first minutes together some of the best.

Talking Through It

How do you balance your family and work time? In what ways is this a struggle for you?

How do you understand covenant related to your relationship with God, your spouse, and your service in the kingdom of God?

In what ways do you presently keep connected with each other? How will these change when you are living separately?

How will you manage conflict when you are apart?

Who will travel for visits and how frequently?

KEEPING INTIMACY ALIVE

J ust being together doesn't connect you as a couple. There are more than a few couples who live as singles under the same roof. Reconnecting during each visit and remaining connected while you are apart is a process, not an event. One couple admitted that the stress of driving many hours to see each other inhibited their physical and emotional intimacy.

Often we think of intimacy in terms of having romantic feelings toward each other. That is only a small part of connecting as intimate partners. Intimacy is the ability to be mutually transparent in a safe, accepting relationship. In healthy intimacy, each person is perceived, conceived, and received with unconditional acceptance and love.

For commuter couples, intimacy can be an issue due to the lack of contact and shared experiences. It's not surprising that couples feel disconnected and perceive that each has changed. Living as singles, each is developing different routines, responsibilities, and interests that are shaping personality and preferences. With the inevitability of change, the particular challenge for commuting couples is to remain connected and intimate.

Emotional Intimacy

Emotional intimacy is the sharing of both positive and negative feelings. Notice I didn't use the words *good* and *bad*. Good and bad are judgmentally charged and it's easy for some to go from having bad feelings to thinking of themselves as being bad. Also, we were taught to be good and avoid bad things. So if certain feelings are labeled as bad, then they are more difficult to acknowledge and accept.

Feelings are neither right nor wrong. They are indicators of how we are responding in a particular moment to our environment and interactions with other people. While we do not choose our feelings, how we react to them is our choice and responsibility.

Connecting emotionally as a couple does not make your spouse responsible for your feelings, nor does it give you permission to dump your negative feelings on your spouse. If you share only your negative feelings, then your spouse becomes a toxic waste dump.

Emotional intimacy is having the freedom and ability to express your feelings without the fear of judgment, rejection, or an attempt by your partner to fix you. When your spouse risks opening up and sharing, be gentle. Avoid trying to correct or negate the feeling by saying something like, "Oh, you shouldn't feel that way." Hear what your partner is saying. If you are clueless as to what is happening, admit it and ask for clarification. Your goal is not to take on the feeling or change the way your partner feels; it is to be present with your partner in the feeling.

Sharing emotional intimacy is risky because of the possibility of rejection or hurt, particularly when expressing negative feelings. By accepting the risk, however, you increase the possibilities of big returns. Some of those returns are knowing each other on a deeper level, experiencing a more genuine love, and being more closely connected as a couple. D. Wayne Matthews adds, "Communication is at the heart of relationships, and feelings are at the heart of effective communication. When we are able to communicate at the feeling level, we can eliminate much of the misunderstandings that occur in most relationships."[22] Communicating at this visceral level is the foundation of every healthy relationship and is integral to staying together while living apart.

Spiritual Intimacy

For clergy couples, spiritual intimacy cannot be assumed. It's sometimes like the plumber's house with leaky faucets, the auto mechanic's car with worn brakes, or the landscaper's yard that needs mowing. It's not a stretch to say that while some pastors' spiritual disciplines—

---

[22] D. Wayne Matthews, "Expressing Feelings", *North Carolina Cooperative Extension Service,* May 1993, Article HE-276-4, http://www.ces.ncsu.edu/depts/fcs/pdfs/fcs2764 (accessed October 15, 2012)

Scripture reading, prayer, meditation and service—are well developed, their spiritual interactions with family are limited. Pastors are good at counseling other couples in the importance of putting God at the center of the marriage relationship, but find that precept more difficult to personally practice. Perhaps for pastors, spirituality has become professionalized, and doing it at home is too much like work.

A question I frequently ask clergy in wellness workshops is, "When do you worship?" Most of them answer that they worship on Sunday morning. I challenge that notion, observing that as pastors, they are leading worship and caring for the spiritual needs of others; it is not a time when their spiritual needs for worship are probably being met.

So when do you and your spouse worship? You both may be in the same worship service on Sunday morning, but one of you is at work. That doesn't seem like a shared spiritual experience.

The most obvious shared experiences are prayer and Scripture reading. Occasionally you may both choose to fast as a spiritual discipline. As with all spiritual disciplines, keep it interesting and engaging by mixing it up. Experiment with different types of prayer: pray the psalms, lectio divina, contemplative prayer, and so on. Change not only the forms, but also the places. For instance, find a new place to walk or hike and pray together. It's energizing!

When you are apart, keeping your spiritual lives connected is more a work of the Spirit. Pray for each other. You may want to read a common devotional, like *The*

Upper Room, and share your insights in an email. One of the most important disciplines to practice is for the nonclergy spouse to attend worship and serve in a local church when not present with your spouse. Your relationship with God needs regular attention to keep it vital and a binding link.

Physical Intimacy

Among the many challenges of a commuter marriage, one that tops the list for many is the lack of physical intimacy. Although couples can talk, Skype, and e-mail to keep connected, it's just not the same as being physically near each other with the ability to touch, smell, and taste as well.

Maintaining physical connection is difficult over the miles. But the other side of the lack of physical contact is gaining an appreciation for the time you spend together and the things you appreciate about each other. Tina Tessina, in an interview with WebMD says, "It's surprisingly good for couples to get a break from each other. Done right, each coming together heightens your appreciation of each other—it's like a mini honeymoon. Being on your own enhances the autonomy of each partner and prevents taking each other for granted. Surprisingly, it often improves communication because you have to be clear when you're at a distance."[23]

---

[23] Suzanne Wright, "Bridging the Distance in a Commuter Marriage", *WebMD Feature*, http://www.webmd.com/sex-relationships/features/bridging-the-distance-in-a-commuter-marriage (accessed November 16, 2012).

The question often arises as to whether there is more infidelity among commuter couples. Although no studies focusing on clergy are available, in the general population, there is no statistical data indicating that the incidence of infidelity increases among commuters. In citing three research studies, Gregory Guldner comments,

> "The good news is that all three studies showed that couples in LDRs [long distance relationships] had no greater risk of having an affair than geographically close couples. It seems that the risk of having an affair is related more to the quality of the relationship between the couple, and the personalities involved, than on mere opportunity."[24]

He goes on to say, however, that among commuting couples there is more worry about their partners having an affair than with those who live together. The key here is the quality of the relationship prior to the separation and the maintenance of the relationship over time and distance.

Physical intimacy is not just about sex; it's about our need for touch and connection with someone. It is well established that infants who receive regular, loving touch gain weight faster, are calmer, sleep longer, and develop better social skills as adolescents. For adults, touch is as important.

---

[24]   Guldner, *Long Distance Relationships*Guldner, 152.

Touch is a conduit of emotions and is capable of conveying the full range of feelings. Like infants who cannot interpret the meaning of words but understand touch, we as adults use touch as a primary language in relationships. In an experiment conducted by Matthew Hertenstein, a psychologist at DePauw University in Indiana, subjects were able to communicate eight distinct feelings to a blindfolded stranger by touch alone, with some 70 percent accuracy.[25]

Touch deprivation can contribute to feeling disconnected, distant, and disinterested. Therefore, as you have opportunity to be together, touching is an important part of reconnecting. Again, this is not sexual touch, although it may go in that direction. It is more holding hands, sitting near each other, and perhaps giving a weary traveling partner a back rub. Touch builds physical intimacy and, more than words, can convey your affection, connection, and devotion to each other.

Developing the art of touch in a relationship deepens the expression of feelings and a sense of connectedness with each other. As couples share this intimacy, it can become a source of heightened awareness of each other and create anticipation when they are apart.

---

[25] Benedict Carey, "Evidence That Little Touches Do Mean So Much," *The New York Times* (February 22, 2010), D5

Talking Through It

How would you rate your intimacy with your partner at this time?

How comfortable are you in expressing your feelings to your partner? How receptive are you to receiving your partner's feelings?

How do you remain spiritually connected with your spouse? Where will the nonclergy spouse attend church?

How important is physical touch in your relationship with your spouse?

In what ways can you keep your marriage alive, intimate, exciting, and forward looking?

WHAT YOUR CONGREGATION NEEDS TO KNOW

Although the leadership and many of the members of your new church know that you and your spouse are living apart, they likely have little understanding of what you are experiencing. Unfortunately, in many congregations the first concern is not about you as a person, but your performance as their pastor. Regardless of your personal situation, they want to see that attendance is increasing, giving is strong, and the worship experiences and program ministries are vital. If these things are happening, then in their collective mind, all is well: you're doing your job. This is true for all pastors, but for you, it may feel like a total disregard for your special circumstances. So what does your congregation need to know?

First, they need to know that you and your spouse made a choice. It's important to clearly state your reasons for living apart, because in the eyes of the congregation, it isn't natural. The standard in our society is that married couples cohabit. You made a choice to live outside of that norm, and people are curious as to why. Some may assume that you are having marital problems. Although you don't owe them an explanation, giving them one will minimize the rumors and give them some clarity into your family dynamic.

In explaining your choice, avoid presenting yourself as a victim. While you may feel that serving under these circumstances is unjust and that it was forced upon you, if you represent this in some way to the congregation, they likely will not respond with sympathy. They may assume that, as you are there against your volition, 1) you really don't want to be there; 2) you have divided loyalties and attention; 3) you will likely be less effective; and 4) you're a short-timer. Any one of these assumptions will make life more difficult for you, and your efficacy will be diminished.

In this light, your congregation needs to know that you are fully present with them. Whatever your tenure, they need the assurance that you are committed to serving them and being with them. Although you may feel you have a heart divided between your family and your congregation, particularly when you first arrive, they want you to integrate your living arrangement and ministry and find a heart united. They desire that you love them and your family fully.

With your congregation's desire for you to succeed in loving them and your family, you need to establish an understanding with the leadership of the church, and even an agreement about the number of days you will spend away visiting your spouse and family. In negotiating this agreement be clear that this is not vacation time; if anything, it's mental health time. Depending on the distance traveled and time commitments required, the number and frequency of those visits differs in each situation. Those in closer proximity may visit more frequently for shorter durations; those with greater distances to travel may visit less often, but for a longer time. Having an agreement with the leadership will give them an awareness of your commitment to your family, avoid the criticism that you're taking too much time away, and give you permission to enjoy some guilt-free time with loved ones.

One question that inevitably comes up is how long you plan to serve that congregation. In the United Methodist Church, clergy are appointed for one year at a time. That is not to suggest that one's tenure is so abbreviated. Rather, it is a block of time defined by the meeting of the annual conference, where the appointments of clergy are read and fixed. In practice, appointments are annually evaluated and usually extended, unless counter indicated, making for a longer time of service in a particular setting. Local leadership is aware of this process and may raise the question of your intentions, whether you plan to stay for only a year or some longer time.

Whether you are appointed for a year at a time or hired indefinitely, the congregation wants to know how long you expect to be with them, particularly if you are living apart from your family. Sometimes implied in their query is really the question, "How long do you think you can do this?" Unless a contract explicitly states the length of your term, the best assurance you can give them is that no matter the duration, you are fully committed to giving them your very best in helping them to become the congregation and people God intends for them to be. No congregation can expect any more or any less than that from you.

One other concern your congregation may have is your emotional health. Generally, people assume that living apart strains the marriage relationship. In most cases, they are genuinely concerned and don't want the arrangement to cause undue stress or damage to your marriage. While maintaining appropriate boundaries, they need your assurance that you are doing the necessary mental health work to minimize the negative impacts of living apart. Then too, they understand that if you and your spouse are not happy, that affects not only your marriage, but also your church work. Sharing with your leadership team or informally with some members a fun experience you and your spouse had during your last visit goes a long way toward reassuring them that domestic tranquility is being maintained.

Talking Through It

What responsibility will you take in informing your congregation of your situation and needs?

What assurances can you give the congregation that you are fully committed to serving them and being in and of the community?

How will you model a healthy marriage for your congregation?

SECTION THREE

LIFE TOGETHER AGAIN

Preparing for
Your Reunion

Acknowledge What You're Leaving

M oving back together under one roof would seem an easy, long overdue homecoming. Yet it's a major adjustment. Laura Stafford says,

> "When couples are separated for extended periods of time, idealization often re-emerges. Positive illusions both serve to sustain a relationship as well as to promote potentially damaging, overly high expectations. Reintegration into the relational and family dynamics involves redefining roles, power structures, and boundary regulations and often encountering unmet expectations. Reunions are tumultuous."[26]

---

[26] Laura Stafford, *Maintaining Long-Distance and Cross-Residential Relationships,* 46.

What can make reunions difficult is that during your time apart, each of you has become more independent and self-directed. You've managed your own schedules, meals, and free time. More importantly, you are not the same people you were before you lived apart.

Before I returned home, Marilyn and I talked about how we had each changed in the two years we were apart. Marilyn had become very self-reliant and handled the operation of our home. She contracted with service technicians to repair broken appliances, supervised the landscaping of our backyard, and did the ordinary chores of keeping a house.

One of her most challenging experiences of autonomy came while driving home from work one evening. Traveling on a four-lane expressway, she signaled her intent to exit. Moving into the off-ramp lane, she began to brake. Immediately every light on her dash lit up, indicating a catastrophic vehicle failure. She had no brakes!

Assessing her choices, she headed for the large exit sign, hoping to stop by striking that instead of the rear end of another vehicle—a crash that could possibly injure the vehicle's occupants. She stopped six feet short of the sign.

Fortunately, a road assistance vehicle was behind her, and its driver soon rendered help. He got her safely off the ramp and into a nearby parking lot, then departed. Shaken, Marilyn called me to tell me her car had died. Thinking she hadn't left the office, I assumed it was her battery at fault and told her she needed to call our road assistance service. Breathless, she then explained what had happened.

She was shaken; I felt helpless. Briefly excusing myself from the Bible class I was teaching, I tried to calm and reassure her. With my guidance, she was able to locate our insurance and towing information in her glove box. She, though, had to take it from there. Marilyn contacted a tow truck, rode in its cab, dropped the car off at the dealership, arranged for a rental car, and cautiously drove home.

Later that night, we reconnected. Knowing she was safe, we were both more at ease. After hanging up, I realized how proud I was of her for her courage, decisiveness, and tenacity. Alone, she handled a major crisis that could have had dire consequences. She became a different woman.

I too changed during those two years. Accustomed to living alone, I had different eating habits, sleeping patterns and work schedules. I was more self-sufficient and learned how to live without a wife. In returning home as you can imagine, some of these changes were for the better and others needed to be dropped, or at least revisited and revised.

In preparing to live together again, there is the need to reflect on what each of you is leaving or losing that is of value. I was leaving my Monday night group, an important part of my social network. Besides the Monday night group, I had formed other relationships in which there was wonderful openness and mutual sharing. Those relationships were reshaped and redefined with my departure. I knew what I was leaving and those to whom I needed to say good-bye.

I was also leaving behind the familiarity and comfort of my routines and church work. I knew what was expected of me, how to do it and how order my time. In reuniting with Marilyn all that changed. I had to create new daily routines and meet new expectations.

For Marilyn, there was the loss of some freedom in her work schedule. With my return, she was more aware of her desire to be home in the evening even with pressing work deadlines. At times this added more stress to her already demanding job.

In honestly appraising what you are leaving, you are better prepared to adjust to the future. As in leaving the security and comfort of living together resulted in feelings of loss, now in returning home there will be other loses to grieve.

Getting Ready to Return

Just as you prepared to set up two homes when you departed, now detailed preparation is needed to return to a single dwelling and life together. Most obvious are the logistics of merging two households of accumulated stuff. During one visit near the end of our time apart, Marilyn and I spent an afternoon going through my Arizona house. We put items in one of four categories: bring home, give to our daughter setting up a home in Denver, take to our vacation home in Vermont, or sell. We created lists and tagged items with a colored dot coded for each destination and purpose. When the move finally came, the decisions were already made, and packing the boxes was easy. We avoided the stress of having to make decisions while packing the boxes or as the movers carried them to the moving truck.

Two consolidations were mine alone: the garage and my clothes. During our time of separation, Marilyn said it was particularly difficult for her to walk into the master bedroom closet and not see any of my clothes hanging there. Thus, on one of my visits home, I brought shirts, pants, jackets, and other clothing to partially fill the closet, my dresser, and her need. One evening when I was home visiting, she came from the master bedroom and declared, "I can see that when you move back, I'm going to need to make some more room in the closet for your things."

It was true. Moving back, I had clothes and shoes in the closet at home, clothes and shoes from my other home, and clothes that were too large, as I had intentionally lost weight while away. Between us, we now fill the master closet and then some, depending on the season.

The other task for me was consolidating and organizing my tools. Inevitably when I visited Marilyn, there were "honey do" jobs. I needed tools for those projects as well as for her occasional use. I also needed tools at my other home for maintenance as well as projects around the church. Then there were the tools three thousand miles away in Vermont. Remembering what was where and anticipating my future needs, I did the best I could to mentally inventory my tools and decide what I needed and where.

In my home away from home, I also had a queen bed in which I fit well, diagonally. One night I was comfortably sleeping when suddenly I felt a movement in my bed. Instantly my mind began processing what was happening. My first thought was that our dog had jumped on the bed; we don't have a dog. Then I thought it was our cats; they were not living with me. I concluded it must be someone broke into the house!

At that moment Marilyn reached over and touched my arm. I screamed and just about jumped out of bed! I was no longer accustomed to having her sleeping with me.

In my return home, one of the adjustments we made was learning to sleep together and share that close space again. We eased the transition by purchasing a California-King bed. Buying the new bed was an acknowledgment of my need for more space and the comfort to which I had become accustomed when sleeping alone.

Sharing space, whether in a closet or a bed, can be a metaphor for mentally and emotionally making room for each other in your lives again. As one pastor said when asked about what surprised him about reuniting, "[It was] much more difficult than I thought it would be. People change, at least a little, every day. After a while those changes add up and if you weren't around for most of the time, then little changes became very significant changes."

There is a time of readjustment to being together and sharing your conjoined lives. Some may experience tension and discord because, living as singles, each partner could always have it his or her way. You made your own decisions and directed your lives separately. Now you need to learn to play together in the same sandbox. There are schedules to coordinate, meals to collaborate and free time to consider. In one sense, it's starting over, only with some history. You are creating a different relationship than you had before you separated.

Talking Through It

In returning home, what relationships, freedoms, and lifestyle patterns are you leaving?

What personal and household items will you consolidate, sell, and give away?

THE NEW YOU

Subtle or pronounced, you are new people returning to cohabitation. During your separation, each of you developed new patterns, habits, and rituals. Taking inventory of these changes and talking about them not only eases the transition, but also may raise your awareness of potential conflicts.

It's not unusual for husbands and wives who have lived apart for a time to look at each other and think, or even say aloud, "You're not the same person." That's true! You are not the same people, and your relationship is not the same either. To imagine that the relationship you once had can be reclaimed is unrealistic. There is no going back in any relationship; there is only your future and the choices you make. In coming together again, you need to reimagine your relationship.

Even before the reality show *Dancing with the Stars*, my wife had wanted us to learn ballroom dancing. That's just not my thing; my sense of beat is like cardiac arrhythmia, and my foot coordination is that of a newborn giraffe trying to stand for the first time. Now that we are reunited, she has restated her wish. While I'm not yet ready to commit, her point about learning to dance is well taken. Being together, we need to learn to be in step with each other and share the movements of life in new ways. If it's not dancing, we still must discover those activities that bring us together for recreation, fun, and learning. These experiences invigorate the mind, body, and spirit, and stimulate the relationship.

Reimagining your relationship is not only about finding common interests and activities, but also dating. From the early days of our courtship and through our years of marriage, Marilyn and I have what we call "date night Friday." As the last day of her work week and my day off, we set aside Friday nights for a date. We go out for dinner and then maybe walk around some shops. Most importantly, we spend time together. When our children were young, they looked forward to date night because they knew fun food, a video, and their favorite babysitter was coming. After more than a couple of decades, we still have our special date night.

Coming back together is a good time to start dating again. Not only is it a great way to get reacquainted and shape your emerging relationship, it's fun! You are making an intentional investment in each other and your relationship. Your date night can be as simple or extravagant as you want to make it. Whether the date is a long walk in the park or a fancy dinner and movie, the most important aspect is spending time together. It's fun to add little surprises such as a secret destination, an evening completely planned by one for the other, flowers, or whatever. Use your imagination to create a wonderful, romantic experience.

Return to Routines

Getting back into the routine of daily living is a challenge. You quickly discover one aspect of your relationship that has changed is role expectations. Before you parted, your roles and responsibilities were well defined and rehearsed. By rote, meals were prepared, dishes washed, garbage taken out, laundry done, house cleaned, yard maintained, et cetera. If children were present, the routines included feeding, homework, bathing, bedtime activities, and discipline. All of these daily rituals were somehow orchestrated.

When you created a second household, these routines were assumed by one person at home and replicated by the other person in the other home (except for the children). Having new roles and responsibilities, you both adapted and adopted routines that worked for you individually. It wasn't necessarily the way things had previously been done. Some things were modified, some were dropped, and others were added for survival and efficiency.

Now reuniting, the spouse coming home is inserted into this modified family system. Asserting old assumptions and role expectations may be perceived as invasive and disruptive for all. This is not a time to assume things will return to the way they were before you lived separately. Assuming the former status quo will cause the greatest woe.

The first months of adjustment to an emerging family system requires patience, grace, and conversation. In my relationship with Marilyn, returning home meant learning a new house and its intricacies, planning and cooking meals, doing laundry, and cleaning the house. Marilyn works five days a week in a corporate office, and I work from home, designing clergy wellness workshops and writing. Having learned a few culinary skills in preparing meals for myself, it was natural for me to flow into making our dinners. Although she loves to cook and bake, she nightly thanks me for having dinner ready when she arrives home. She works her wonders in the kitchen on the weekends.

Other household chores are likewise shared with me taking the lead on many of them so we have our weekends free to enjoy a variety of activities and pleasures. What we had done solo for two years, we are now harmonizing, each with his or her own part complementing the other. We're creating new routines and roles that work for us as a couple, as well as discovering new things we enjoy doing together.

In returning to a single household, you will be creating a new family system. The returning spouse needs to spend time learning the existing system before imposing any personal methods. It is similar to going to a new church. With the arrival of a new pastor, the congregation expects some change in the way things are done. But implementing radical changes, such as different worship times or styles, without first understanding why and how things are currently done and getting some consensus and support for the changes, can result in conflict and a difficult transition.

The changes that took place during the time of separation became a part of the family system. Some are functional and others dysfunctional, but all are part of the dynamic. To ignore or discount those rituals or roles is to invite conflict. If change is prematurely introduced, there will likely be resistance and the sentiment of "But you weren't here!"

Take the time as a couple to learn what has changed in the house and why it changed. Then evaluate whether it is still viable for the future. Just as in the church, simply saying, "We've always done it that way," isn't productive in forming your new family system. Discovering and working toward your new roles and identity as a couple requires willingness to understand and change, even when it's uncomfortable.

Some would say this transition requires a great deal of compromise. While compromise is one element in negotiating your new roles, I suggest another paradigm. In compromise, there are elements of give and take that are healthy, but compromise can also be perceived as a game of winners and losers. To settle a difference, one side may give more than the other, and there is no meeting in the middle. If this consistently happens, the one who gives in may start keeping score. At an opportune time to even the score, the one who has counted the number of times he or she has given in will demand his or her way. When couples begin keeping score and stating, "You owe me," conflict is inevitable.

Rather than a bartering model in which there can be perceived winners and losers, think in terms of both of you winning. Rather than a scale that tips to one side or the other, an image for this paradigm is intersecting circles whose degree of overlap may change. The area of intersection represents those relationship elements that are shared, whether those are roles, interests, or expectations. The goal is to constantly grow this area of intersection.

A point of difference is brought into the common area by a partner expanding his or her circle to include it. This represents the spouse making that point part of his or her awareness. In growing the middle, one circle is enlarged to encompass the interest of the other without giving up something in return. The other circle is not diminished in size by the enlargement of the other, but itself grows in size by feeling valued, validated, and loved. Both circles are enlarged, the area of intersection is enlarged, and the relationship is enlarged. In this paradigm, one person didn't win and the other lose; rather both won and both grew.

Using this new paradigm doesn't mean that there is always agreement and harmony. Rather, by enlarging the circle, there is the opportunity for continuing the conversation about difference and sometimes coming to a place of accepting that there will not be agreement. Even without agreement, if love and respect for each other is affirmed and maintained, there is not a winner and a loser. Both of you win!

Your New Normal

As you are not who you were as a couple, you are creating for yourselves what will become your new normal. You are becoming a new creation, a new couple with a new future. Your goal in reconnecting is not to recreate what once was, but together find what is becoming normal for the two of you.

After about a year, Marilyn and I are settling into a comfortable pattern. A significant part of our adjustment in finding a new normal is adjusting to my not working in the local church. There are no evening meetings, no emergency calls and no Sunday responsibilities. Our time is our own, which is radically different for us and especially for me. It is part of *living into* our new normal.

A new normal is not the attainment of a static state, but rather the ability to change and accommodate each other's needs and an ever-fluid reality. In biological science, this is called *homeostasis*. Our bodies are constantly adjusting to maintain a constant core temperature, essential levels of water, salt, sugar, proteins, and myriad other vital conditions to keep us alive. In returning to a life as couple and finding a new normal, your goal is not to set rigid standards and roles, but to be aware of changing needs and adjust accordingly. Therefore, your new normal two years from now may be radically different than it is at present. A new normal is your commitment to a dynamic process that, when done well, builds intimacy and a stronger, more durable relationship.

Talking Through It

How have you changed during your time apart? How do you perceive your partner has changed?

What adjustments do you perceive as necessary in reuniting? How will you negotiate your new roles? Describe your new normal.

SECTION FOUR

FROM THE SPOUSE'S PERSPECTIVE

BY MARILYN MATTICK

IN HER OWN WORDS

When Tom and I married, I accepted that it was my role to be the "trailing" spouse. As a United Methodist minister, Tom is part of the itinerant system and thou shalt go where the Bishop sends you. My career in human resources as a compensation professional would be subjugated to Tom's. This was part of the package in deciding to marry Tom, and it was a small price for my daughter and me to pay to marry the love of my life.

Each year as the appointive season drew near, there was some level of anxiety in our lives. Even if we did not expect a move or request a move, a move could come. It was a tough time of year. The questions that I pondered included:

- Is this the year we will move?
- Where will we go?
- Where will we live?
- How hard will it be to sell our house?
- What will the effect be on the children?
- Will the schools be fulfilling and challenging?

- Will I be able to find a comparable position in my career field?

Going into the 2010 appointive season was different; we knew in November 2009 that Tom would be moved. The new church start that he was serving could no longer support a full-time pastor. It was different because we knew that if Tom was moved out of the Las Vegas valley, he would be moving alone. I had reached a point in my career that I was at the executive level, and to leave that position would cause us great financial consequences. Even a move to one of the other major cities in our conference, Phoenix or Tucson, would cause the same result. Tom would be moving alone.

I never, ever thought that my career would be this important and financially rewarding; I am grateful for my profession and position.

Getting Ready To Living Apart

The waiting was difficult. Where would Tom be appointed? Would a church open up in Las Vegas that would match his gifts and graces? We could not plan, we could not move forward, until we knew.

The call finally came in late April: Lake Havasu City, 150 miles away. Damn.

The all-out sprint started. We had little time to find a place for Tom to live, provide furnishings for that house from a bed to toilet paper, and arrange for the movers. As Tom was on a sabbatical leave, this became his full-time job. I helped when I could, selecting what from our current house he could take with him and what was to be purchased. Buying furniture seemed surreal, and picking out dishes with an eye for something neutral felt like a huge chore. We were consumed with getting him ready to go, and I felt left out. I wasn't going. We would no longer be living together.

Part of the getting ready process was to assess how I would maintain our current house, from what tools I would need to how to deal with the pool and lawn. This overwhelmed me.

We talked about how often I would go to Lake Havasu and how often he would come home. It was clear from the start that it was unrealistic for me to travel to Lake Havasu every weekend. Working long hours during the week and on occasional weekends, I would have no down time to do the usual weekend chores, visit our daughter who lives the area, or just vegetate. We agreed that I would visit every other weekend.

The furnishings were acquired, the plans were made, but nothing prepared me for the reality of Tom leaving, moving away, and not spending time together each day.

Living Apart

The finality of living apart really hit home when, at the end of our annual conference, the bishop read the names of the pastors and the churches they were to serve for the ensuing year. That first year when Tom's name was read, I cried. No, I sobbed. At the end of the worship service, when I knew the time was near that Tom would be driving to his new home in Lake Havasu City, Arizona and I would be flying home to Las Vegas, neither of us wanted to talk to anyone. We quietly fled through a side door. It was no better the second year; in fact, I felt it was worse, as there was no end in sight.

My first visit to Lake Havasu City was fun. Tom was so proud of how he had set up his house and explored his new community, and he was anxious to share it with me. I appreciated the little touches he added to make me feel that this was my home as well. But at the end of the weekend, it was very difficult to part yet again, and again and again over the next two years.

Through it all, Tom's church was very welcoming and accepting of our living situation. Still, I felt like a visitor, not a member and not the pastor's wife. After years of being a pastor's wife, I felt like I didn't have a church home. On the weekends that I stayed in Las Vegas, I occasionally went to church, but I felt like I didn't belong there either. After a period of time, I did not go to church at all except when I was with Tom.

My life changed in many ways while we lived apart. Yes, I was married, but I felt very alone. The first year I went on vacation with family as Tom was not able to get away. I attended the necessary company functions alone, without Tom. I went to special events for family and friends alone, without Tom.

My day-to-day routine changed. With nothing waiting for me at home except two hungry cats, I worked longer and longer hours with little regard to the time. When I did get home, evenings were spent knitting prayer shawls, watching "girly" television, and Skyping with Tom. One of the benefits of working in the hospitality industry in Las Vegas is being provided with a free lunch. I quickly established that lunch would be my main meal of the day and had a very light dinner or snack in the evening.

I also established the routine of doing errands on the way home from work, particularly when I would not be home the coming weekend. In a sense, I developed more of an independent spirit than I already had. I controlled my schedule and did not have to worry about anyone else's schedule.

Home repairs were all on me to coordinate. The air conditioning went out twice the first summer. The new pool service was constantly failing to secure the gate and leaving things behind besides the bill. I had to select a new pest control service to take care of "my friends" the scorpions when we moved to our new house on the other side of town. Coordinating that service was very unreliable at first. Then there were the appliance repairs that needed to be handled, and I certainly cannot forget the frightening night I lost my car brakes on I-215. Tom handled the routine repairs when he was able to come home, but these emergencies felt overwhelming at times and made me appreciate even more the flexible schedule Tom had had to handle all of these issues when we lived together.

It was the passing of a friend, Tim, at the beginning of our second year apart that caused me to question how long we could sustain a commuter marriage. Tim was married to my dear friend Linda, and Linda not only mourned the passing of her beloved husband at age sixty-two, but the passage of time and putting off things that they had wanted to do together "someday."

This event made me keenly aware of the years that Tom and I were spending apart. We could not get them back; they were lost. This also reminded me that Tom is older than I, and that my mother passed away at age seventy-five from Alzheimer's. I feared the potential of more lost years. I wanted to live my life with my husband.

One of the unexpected joys during our time living apart was having my father escape the cold Vermont winter during the second year and come to stay with me for three months. He traveled with me to Lake Havasu City and also spent a week there with Tom. I treasured this time with my dad, knowing that this was probably a once-in-a-lifetime opportunity to be together like that. We shared so much during those three months about his life, especially his life with my mother. There were lots of laughs and lots of tears. I truly thank God for the gift of that time with my dad.

The other aspect of Dad's visit was it started preparing me for living with Tom again.

Coming Back Together

Another appointment season came around in 2012, and this time the joyous news was that Tom was coming home!

Logistics quickly became the priority again, primarily to do with his household goods: what goes to which child, what goes to our lake house in Vermont, and what comes home with him. Being the organized people that we are, Tom quickly developed a system and handled all the aspects of the move home.

One of my concerns with Tom coming home was, "How do I help transition him to accept our new house as not only my home, but his home as well?" We had to decide where we would put his stuff, and I had to make sure he understood that we could move anything around to accommodate his stuff, my stuff, and our stuff.

This was followed by the reality that the routine I had established for myself was going to change, and I needed to be flexible. I was also concerned that during the two years apart, we had learned how to live apart, and now we had to learn how to live together again.

Tom came home the third week in June, but with the annual conference, summer vacation, and our daughter's wedding in Denver, we didn't really start living together and developing a daily routine until early August. Then, if adjusting to living together wasn't enough, we lost our minds and adopted a twelve-week-old golden doodle puppy. So much change!

Coming back together and living together was a process, as we were in some ways different people, and our previous routines needed to be altered. My work schedule was now the one that we benchmarked meals and other activities off of, and this was a major change from working around Tom's schedule at the local church.

Another change was household responsibilities. As Tom began working from home on his clergy wellness ministry, he agreed that he would be responsible for the evening meals during the week. He also cleaned the house, which had become a much bigger chore with the arrival of the puppy. Friday nights have always been date night, and then I took over the cooking on the weekend.

In my position, I am not always able to leave at the end of the workday at a set time. With Tom home, I began the practice of trying to give him enough notice that I was stuck in a meeting, on a conference call, or on a project so that he would not begin to prepare dinner. I always call him when I get to my car, which gives him a thirty-minute countdown to my arrival. Knowing that he is home during the day, I try to call him at midday and touch base. How wonderful it is knowing that when we talk on the telephone now, he is a few miles away and not 150.

The ability to do errands together is simply a joy. Yes, there are times that I want to do some shopping on my own, and I make time for that as well. I still knit prayer shawls in the evening, but not at the pace that I did while we were apart. And I don't take for granted the pleasure of waking up beside my husband in the morning or holding his hand when we take a walk in the evening. I treasure every moment that I have with him.

Coming back together after living apart for two years has been a journey that continues. The biggest keys to success are being aware of each other's needs, communicating, being committed to the process, and being committed to each other.

SECTION FIVE

CONCLUDING REMARKS

SEEING THE LARGER PICTURE

T ime and distance often add perspective to life. In a commuter marriage, there is the opportunity to take inventory of yourself and the relationship you share with your spouse. Often you can see things you have not seen before. You appreciate some of those and realize there is the need to change others.

For a time, I had a private pilot's license and an airplane. Each time I flew, even over familiar routes, I enjoyed the view from above. Being four to eight thousand feet above the terrain, I could see the big picture of the mountains dropping into the valleys, the rivers meandering through the desert, and the highways carrying a flow of traffic from one town to the next. The relationship between desert landscapes and populated cities in the West was much more obvious from above. From the air, I saw the same topography as when driving it, but from a larger, different perspective.

Living in a commuter marriage gives you the opportunity to gain new perspectives on your life that you are not otherwise afforded. You may see how things are fitting or not fitting together for you. In seeing yourself and your relationships from a new vantage point, you can realize what is really important and what is not.

These revelations and new insights are all growth opportunities, whether confirmations of what is good in life or convictions of what needs to change in you personally, your marriage, or your family dynamic. Just as in flying, you can appreciate this different perspective, but at some point you need to extend the landing gear and touch down on terra firma. What you have seen and heard and experienced is now a part of who you are.

If you set your mind on it and if you let it, even under the less than optimal circumstances of a commuter marriage, "We know that all things work together for good for those who love God, who are called according to his purpose."[27] Let the good prevail.

---

[27] Romans 8:28.

APPENDIX A

ONLINE DEPRESSION INVENTORIES

CES-D: http://counsellingresource.com/lib/quizzes/depression-testing/cesd/
> Center for Epidemiological Studies Depression Scale (CES-D)—20 questions
> This quick self-test measures depressive feelings and behaviors during the past week.

Goldberg: http://counsellingresource.com/lib/quizzes/depression-testing/goldberg-depression/
> Dr. Ivan K. Goldberg—18 questions
> This inventory highlights the sign and symptoms of depression.

K10: http://counsellingresource.com/lib/quizzes/depression-testing/depression-anxiety/
> Clinical Research Unit for Anxiety and Depression—10 questions

This scale includes signs and symptoms
of anxiety related to depression.

Mayo Clinic: http://www.mayoclinic.com/health/
depression/MH00103_D
Drs. Robert Spitzer, Janet Williams, and
Kurt Kroenke—9 questions
This self-assessment can indicate the need
for treatment for depression.

QIDS-SR: http://counsellingresource.com/lib/quizzes/
depression-testing/qids-depression/
Quick Inventory of Depressive
Symptomatology—16 questions
This instrument measures the severity of depression.

Wakefield: http://counsellingresource.com/lib/quizzes/
depression-testing/wakefield/
University of Leeds—12 questions
This self-test screens for symptoms of major depression.